1963

THE
POETIC THEORY OF PAUL VALÉRY

INSPIRATION AND
TECHNIQUE

THE POETIC THEORY
OF PAUL VALÉRY

INSPIRATION AND
TECHNIQUE

by

W. N. INCE

M.A., Docteur de l'Université de Paris

Lecturer in French in the University of Leicester

LEICESTER UNIVERSITY PRESS

1961

TO
MY FATHER AND MOTHER

PREFACE

THIS book is a modified version of a thesis presented in 1955 for the *doctorat de l'université de Paris*.

I wish to express my warm appreciation of the help I have received in my work. Professor Pierre Moreau and Professor Octave Nadal gave me the benefit of their encouragement and counsel. Madame Valéry, with great kindness, allowed me to consult at her home all the typed copies she has of the lectures on poetics which Valéry gave at the *Collège de France*. I am most grateful to her for authorizing me to quote from them (They extend from November 1937 to March 1938, twenty-nine lectures in all; unfortunately, she has no record of the lectures given between 1938 and 1945). I wish to thank Madame Leduc for letting me see the notes she took during lectures after March 1938. To Professor P. Mansell Jones I am grateful for some valuable suggestions. To Professor L. C. Sykes I owe a special debt: he read my manuscript and gave me much useful advice on the presentation of my material. For the faults that remain, I am alone responsible. My thanks are also due to Leicester University Press for publishing this book and to the General Editor of *French Studies* for permission to reproduce certain pages published in that journal.

W.N.I.

Leicester, 26 January 1960

CONTENTS

Preface   vii

Introduction   1

Chapter   I   The change of attitude from youth to maturity   11

   II   Mind and Body   35

   III   Poetry and the reader   64

   IV   The stages of poetic creation   95
     I   Preparation   96
     II   Illumination   117
     III   Composition: The poet at work   129

Conclusion: 'personal inspiration'   164

Index   183

INTRODUCTION

THE history of the notion of *inspiration*, taken in its broadest implications, can scarcely be dissociated from the history of thought itself. Explanations of it vary according to the theory of art and the epistemology prevalent at the time. But as regards the experience itself, the area of agreement is considerable. Inspiration has been thought to embrace some or all of the following cases:

1. Creation is involuntary and automatic.
2. Creation occurs suddenly, without effort.
3. During creation, the poet experiences great excitement, felt either as pleasurable or painful, but, even when painful, almost always leading to a pleasurable sense of relief when composition is finished.
4. A sense of alienation in the poet who cannot recognize what he has written as his own work.[1]

From ancient times up to the seventeenth century, art was, largely speaking, seen as mimetic, through the influence of Plato and Aristotle. As the critic's attention was mostly concentrated on the reality which was imitated or on the work which was the imitator, there was little subtle analysis of poetic invention. The poet was thought to be the recipient of an external and supernatural afflatus, a frenzy, a madness. Plato wrote:

All the epic poets, the good ones, utter all their beautiful poems not through art but because they are divinely inspired and possessed, and the same is true of the good lyric poets . . .[2]

[1] For a number of ideas and facts in the early part of this introduction, we are indebted to M. H. Abrams's excellent book, *The Mirror and the Lamp: Romantic Theory and the Critical Tradition*, New York, Oxford University Press, 1953.

[2] *Ion*, and quoted under *inspiration* in Shipley's *Dictionary of World Literary Terms*, London, Allen and Unwin, 1955.

The Horatian tradition, however, gave a different emphasis. A distinction was made between the nature of the poet, comprehending the feeling and imagination which were his special birthright, and the art of the poet, something to be learned and acquired with effort. These two aspects, which together form the basis of the neo-classic tradition, maintained a not always comfortable alliance well into the seventeenth century. To this tradition, many aspects of the mechanical laws associated with Newton and the physical sciences had been annexed by the beginning of the next century. Ideas were now thought to be the constituent elements of artistic invention, and they were all derived from initial sense impressions; ideas were merely fainter replicas of sense impressions. Artistic invention was a process whereby the basic elements, ideas, were re-arranged according to certain laws of mental association. It was natural, with such a background, that the purposive and conscious aspects of creation should be stressed, though a residue of the old belief in poetic afflatus remained, not easily assimilable, through the current notions of the *je ne sais quoi* and what Pope called "a grace beyond the reach of art."[1] The prevailing emphasis might be summed up by another quotation from Pope: "True ease in writing comes from art, not chance."[2]

Gradually, in the course of the eighteenth century, the pendulum in literary criticism swung away from art, judgement, purposive and deliberate creation, towards feeling, emotion, imagination, 'inspired' creation. As is well known, battle was joined in the second half of the century between the defenders of 'art' and the defenders of 'nature'. By the end of the century, poets and critics were concerned primarily with the feeling, the passion, the rapture, to be experienced through poetry. The lyric poem was given pride of place. The centre of interest in literary discussion inevitably shifted from the poem to the poet, since the mimetic aspect of art was in abeyance and attention was now concentrated on an organic

[1] *Essay on Criticism.*
[2] *Ibid.*

creative process. The equation of feeling with poetry is perhaps expressed in its most extreme form by Hazlitt when he writes: "Fear is poetry, hope is poetry, love is poetry, hatred is poetry."[1]

Many would contest the notion that there is one romantic conception of poetic invention, but on some points at least most of the romantics, French or English, seem to agree. Thus, they see an opposition between reason or intelligence, associated with judgement and deliberate, conscious effort, and feeling or passion, associated with involuntary composition. They usually assume that the man with intense feeling is a poet or as near being a poet as makes no difference. The idea of the natural genius was wide-spread, fostered by poets and critics (how deliberately, for propaganda purposes, it is difficult to say): the genius is the man of feeling who is connected in a special way with some transcendental power. Shelley's reference to poetry as "planetary music"[2] is characteristic. The phrase and the notion behind it are essentially Platonic: poetry is a vision or experience of the eternal Forms, which the poet merely transmits. Thus Blake could declare, of his Milton:

I have written this Poem from immediate Dictation, twelve or sometimes twenty or thirty lines at a time, without Premeditation and even against my Will.[3]

The dictating, transcendental power could be envisaged as a god or muse; but more commonly, as the organic view of creation grew in importance, it was seen as the unconscious, the repository of the 'natural' in man:

The definition of genius is that it acts unconsciously; and those who have produced immortal works have done so without knowing how or why . . .[4]

[1] Quoted by Abrams, op. cit., p. 154.
[2] A Defence of Poetry, in Shelley's Prose, edited by D. L. Clark, Albuquerque, The University of New Mexico Press, 1954, p. 282.
[3] Quoted by Abrams, op. cit., p. 215.   [4] Ibid. The words are Hazlitt's.

For in all vital things, men distinguish an Artificial and a Natural ... the artificial is the conscious, mechanical, the natural is the unconscious, dynamical.[1]

An important aspect of the romantic conception of poetic creation seems to derive ultimately from an early fusion of Platonic and Plotinian theory. In Plato, the artist is reduced to being a copier of a reality which is itself a copy of eternal Ideas or Forms. Plotinus vindicated the artist's rôle by stressing that art imitates rather the eternal Ideas which inhabit the mind, and is therefore able to reflect the transcendental better than the universe about us. The further deduction, that no beauty of any actual work of art can equal that in the mind, from which it is copied, is at the heart of the romantic conception of poetry as expounded, for instance, by Shelley in his *Defence of Poetry* or as implied by a Lamartine or a Hugo. The latter wrote in his *Préface de Cromwell* that "le génie est nécessairement inégal" :[2] inevitably, the poetic genius cannot do full justice on paper to the wonderful vision or experience he has been given. It is in the nature of things that he should write speedily, involuntarily, very excitedly, to get as much on paper as he can before the vision or experience fades. A premium is thus set on improvisation, spontaneous utterance which is seen as necessarily imperfect, but without doubt the best that can be achieved by mortals, given its transcendental origin.

A series of terms can thus be marshalled which, with the various nuances accorded them by different writers, convey the polarity of inspiration and technique. At one pole, the characteristic words are: feeling, emotion, passion, rapture, natural, unconscious, dynamic, immediate, imaginative; at the other: reason, intellect, art, judgement, conscious, and the two pejoratives, artificial and mechanical. The two groups represent views of poetic creation each of which has tended to try to oust the other and which have enjoyed varying fortunes and

[1] *Ibid.*, p. 217. The words are Carlyle's.
[2] *La Préface de Cromwell*, edited by Maurice Souriau, Boivin, Paris, no date, p. 321.

come together in different compositions according to the individual and the current epistemology. Romantic poets, particularly French ones, were not on the whole notable for their analyses and explanations of the poetic process. Their adherence to the views implicit in the first group makes them disinclined to analyse, and certainly, incapable of analysing well. Coleridge, of course, is the most striking exception.

Valéry reacted strongly against the romantic view of poetic creation, in a way which perhaps seems inevitable to us now, because of his antecedents and his own nature. He inherited the post-romantic tradition, that of such poets as Baudelaire and Mallarmé, not to mention Heredia, which gave intelligent emphasis to both the aspects of creation we have indicated, either of which had been embraced too exclusively by many previous poets. His dominant desire was to understand by analysis and reflection: he found many of the notions of previous generations naïve, vague, confused and too partisan. We shall see that Valéry began as an anti-romantic, an upholder of the notions implied in our second group of terms. As a young man, he is as partisan as many romantic poets, and (some might argue) not much less naïve and confused than they were. More understanding, wisdom and subtlety came to him with age.

*

We need to define briefly the two key words in the title of this study. *Technique* can mean the mode of execution in a given art and refers to whatever can be envisaged as methodical, structural, reducible to formulae; it signifies, in short, mastery of one's craft or art, knowledge of one's materials as revealed by the mode of execution. There is no necessary opposition between *technique* and *inspiration; technique* can be seen as complementary to the latter. A poet can be seen as having a *technique* and relying on *inspiration*: his *technique* would then be, for the most part, involuntary and unconscious, and composition easy and swift. Yet the word *technique* is partly defined in the *Oxford Dictionary* as "mechanical skill in art": the word *mechanical*, probably used somewhat pejoratively here, seems to imply that the best poetry must owe a great debt to a vitalistic force, *inspiration*. This force is thought to produce a largely involuntary and unconscious *technique* with speedy composition, and it is implied that a *technique* consciously applied must produce a kind of inferior art because it involves an unoriginal, automatic application of known formulae. In this study, involuntary and unconscious *technique* will be classed as a product of *inspiration*, and when the word *technique* is used, willed and conscious "mechanical skill in art" will usually be intended. Thus, for our purposes, *technique* might be defined as, ideally, the exact opposite of *inspiration;* it will refer to the means whereby the poet composes poetry using his will and reason, consciously controlling himself and his medium, language.

Some views on inspiration have already been mentioned. But in order to follow Valéry's thought we need sharper definitions. For him, the word can mean any one of six things:

1.   The dictation sometimes of a whole poem by a supernatural power; this is just what, as we have seen, it meant for Blake. The supernatural power can be a god, as in the 'verbal inspiration' of the Scriptures, a muse envisaged as external to the poet, the nineteenth-century 'unconscious', or the twentieth-century god, the 'subconscious'. This sort of inspiration will be referred to throughout this study as 'total inspiration'.

2.   What Valéry calls the "état poétique."[1] This state is not confined to the person who actually composes poems, and therefore does not necessarily find expression in a poem, or even in words. In fact, Valéry conceives the state as the essential experience which all the arts,—poetry, music, painting and architecture—derive from and seek to recreate in their various ways for those to whom they are addressed. The state is a "certain genre d'émotion:"[2] it is

> entièrement indépendant de toute œuvre déterminée et il résulte naturellement et spontanément d'un certain accord

---

[1] *Propos sur la poésie, Conf.*, p. 65.
[2] *Calepin d'un poète*, in *Poésies*, p. 202.

entre notre disposition intime, physique et psychique, et les circonstances (réelles ou idéales) qui nous impressionnent.[1]

His notion, based upon his own experience, is that this state can occur during certain periods of our life which might be loosely described as *poetic*. This form of inspiration will be referred to as 'intermittent inspiration'.

3. In the third place, inspiration can be an illumination, a flash of insight. This form of inspiration presupposes that the poet is in one of the poetic "periods" just mentioned. Thus it is closely connected with 'intermittent inspiration'; the main difference between the two is that the "poetic state" or "poetic emotion" is experienced by persons who do not necessarily become artists or composers of poems. Illumination might be defined as occurring at one of those privileged moments of the "poetic state" in which it suddenly gives certain verbal or rhythmical "fragments"; it visits a person so gifted and so formed that it suddenly gives rise to a *trouvaille* which he will be able to profit by for the purpose of composing a poem. Briefly, we shall be concerned with two forms of illumination. The first is the original illumination which makes the poet start writing a poem, or think about starting to write a poem; this may be an emotion which calls for expression in words or a rhythm which obsesses him until it is clothed with words. The second is the illumination or flash of insight which occurs during actual composition. This second type is the consequence of exigencies and conditions different from those governing the first.

It goes without saying that either form of illumination may result in *trouvailles* which the poet may put on one side to explore further, or to incorporate in their original form into the poem at some later stage. Whichever type it is, this illumination seems perhaps the nearest to what is most commonly thought of as inspiration. In the following pages it will be designated as 'intuitive inspiration', either 'primary' or 'secondary'.

[1] *Ibid.*, p. 203.

4. A fourth form of inspiration is a state of exaltation. This does not imply loss of self-control. On the contrary, in this usually pleasurable state of elation, excitement, when ideas or words crowd in upon him, the poet feels a supreme assurance in his powers. He works and composes often at speed and with an excited tension. Coleridge describes moments which are characterized by "judgement ever awake and steady self-possession, with enthusiasm and feeling profound or vehement."[1] Like 'intuitive inspiration', this form is closely connected with 'intermittent inspiration', and apparently presupposes it. But it is not just 'intermittent inspiration', partly for the same reasons as those which led us to differentiate between the 'intuitive' and 'intermittent' forms; not is it just 'intuitive inspiration', since the latter gives only brief flashes of insight. It is, so to speak, the "poetic state" wedded to poetic composition. The expression 'exalted inspiration' will be used to denote this form of inspiration.

5. Inspiration may, fifthly, represent a value-judgement by the reader who uses the word to describe that state which the poet must, he thinks, have experienced to write such good poetry. This form of inspiration is summed up by Valéry thus:

L'inspiration est, positivement parlant, une attribution gracieuse que le lecteur fait à son poète: le lecteur nous offre les mérites transcendants des puissances et des grâces qui se développent en lui. Il cherche et trouve en nous la cause merveilleuse de son émerveillement.[2]

The phrase 'attributed inspiration' will be used to indicate such a state.

6. The last meaning which inspiration can have is that of

[1] *Biographia Literaria*, Chapter XIV, London, Oxford University Press, 1949, Vol. II, p. 12.

[2] *Poésie et pensée abstraite*, in *Var. V*, p. 138. Cf. Sir Maurice Bowra, *Inspiration and Poetry* (Rede lecture delivered at Cambridge in 1951), London, Macmillan, 1955, p. 3: "But when we say that a modern poem is inspired, we mean that it is of an unusual excellence in a special way. We assume that inspiration accounts not so much for a poem's existence as for its worth."

an inspiring principle—the themes, emotions and tones pecul-
iar to the poet, the personal something which distinguishes
him from other men. This meaning takes no account of the way
the poet makes his contribution, how he works, or whether the
poetry he produces is controlled or inspired in any of the first
four senses given above. It includes what Valéry once called
the "champ métaphysique" of the poet[1] and will be referred
to in this study as 'personal inspiration'.

*

It is possible to find among poets every conceivable attitude
from complete acceptance of 'total inspiration' to complete
rejection of inspiration in our first four senses.

> I can aver [says Herbert Read], that all the poetry I have
> written which I continue to regard as authentic poetry was
> written immediately, instantaneously, in a condition of
> trance.[2]

Yet William Morris writes:

> That talk of inspiration is sheer nonsense; there is no such
> thing. It is a mere matter of craftsmanship.[3]

But most poets seem to occupy a position somewhere between
these two extremes. Some confess that, as might indeed be
expected, the degree of inspiration has varied from poem to
poem. Many poets seem to have known 'intermittent',
'intuitive' or 'exalted inspiration' in some form or other, and
to have recognized, if only by implication, the presence of
'personal inspiration'.

Valéry reveals his thoughts concerning inspiration and technique in writings often repetitious and occasionally incoherent.
Our purpose will be to organize a comprehensive account of
his theories. Though influences on Valéry and weaknesses in
his views will concern us to some extent, our ambition will not

---

[1] *La Création artistique*, in *Vues*, p. 287.
[2] *Collected Essays in Literary Criticism*, Faber, 1938, p. 110.
[3] Quoted by Bowra, *op. cit.*, p. 2.

be to deal with them closely and systematically. Nor will it be our chief aim to examine what rôle inspiration and technique played in the poetry which he himself wrote, though this aspect cannot be completely ignored since he theorizes from personal experience. We shall be mostly preoccupied to discover to what extent work and effort are responsible for a finished poem, how conscious and controlled the act of poetic creation is or can be according to Valéry. No poet we know of matches him in the subtle distinctions with which he examines the various stages of poetic composition and the various implications of the idea of inspiration.

THE CHANGE OF ATTITUDE FROM YOUTH TO MATURITY

VALERY's attitude to the dichotomy which concerns us was not the same in 1940 as it was in 1890. In his early youth, he reveals a more or less intransigent rejection of inspiration (with the various aspects not differentiated as in later years), allied to a complete confidence in technique and its powers. In his maturity, his attitude reveals more subtlety; he still puts as much emphasis as possible on conscious control and knowledge, but recognizes the limits of technique and the inevitability, even the desirability, of all forms of inspiration except 'total inspiration'.

The complete confidence the young Valéry had in technique is disclosed by the article *Sur la technique littéraire*,[1] submitted to the *Courrier libre* in 1889, but not published until 1946. Fired by his reading of Poe, he writes in this article:

> La littérature est l'art de se jouer de l'âme des autres ... Etant donnés une impression, un rêve, une pensée, il faut l'exprimer de telle manière qu'on produise dans l'âme d'un auditeur le maximum d'effet—et un effet entièrement calculé par l'Artiste.

In terms which sometimes recall the *Epilogue* of Verlaine's *Poèmes Saturniens*, the nineteen-year-old theorist dismisses inspirational writing such as is found in many romantics:

> [le poète] se gardera de jeter sur le papier tout ce que lui soufflera aux minutes heureuses la Muse Association-des-Idées. Mais, au contraire, tout ce qu'il aura imaginé, senti, songé, échafaudé, passera au crible, sera pesé, épuré, mis à la *forme* et condensé le plus possible pour gagner en force ce qu'il sacrifie en longueur ...

[1] Published by Henri Mondor in *Le premier article de Paul Valéry*, pp. 13–20 of *Dossiers*, Paris, Janin, July 1946.

He writes with youthful enthusiasm of

> une conception toute nouvelle et moderne du poète. Ce n'est plus le délirant échevelé, celui qui écrit tout un poème dans une nuit de fièvre, c'est un froid savant, presque un algébriste, au service d'un rêveur affiné.

Praising Poe's *Philosophy of Composition*, he observes that

> aucune de ses œuvres ne renferme plus d'acuité dans l'analyse, plus de rigueur dans le logique développement des principes découverts par l'observation. C'est une technique entière-ment *a posteriori*, établie sur la psychologie de *l'auditeur*, sur la connaissance des diverses notes qu'il s'agit de faire résonner dans l'âme d'autrui.

Several important points thus emerge from this article. His ironic reference to "la Muse Association-des-Idées" shows by implication that, even if he could at this stage believe in inspiration, he could not think of it as a gift from the gods, some force from outside the poet. We all have feelings, ideas, imagination, but these define any man, not the poet. Association of ideas cannot give us fine poems. 'Total inspiration' is clearly dismissed. It is the technique of the poet, the "froid savant, presque un algébriste," which, by the form, the arrangement it gives to ideas and feelings, creates poetry. There are certain principles which can be deduced from observation and which, as with Poe, constitute the poet's technique. But we are not given details of these principles; Valéry has more faith than knowledge at this stage. Already we see in germ the attitude and some of the principles which the later Valéry will develop and expound in much greater detail—in particular, the distinc-tion between poet, poem and reader, and the importance attached to the psychological side of art.

Valéry is very much a young man of his time, and art is almost a religion for him.[1] To Mallarmé, in 1891, he writes that

---

[1] Cf. *Cahiers, tome sixième*, p. 25: "Une génération 'formée par le culte du beau'. Ceci n'est pas ironie. Je note un fait—que je vois: un moment dont j'ai fait partie. Le rôle joué par l'idée vague et intense de 'Beauté' sur

poetry seems to him "une explication du Monde délicate et belle."[1] He is something of an aesthete in these early years; he puts into the pursuit and veneration of the means of poetic expression much of the idealism and passion which earlier generations of poets in the nineteenth century had put into the content of their lives and poetry. The period is technique-minded, as he will point out in *Existence du Symbolisme;* poets and artists are technique-minded with passion, as Valéry is, bent on the transcendentalism of the aesthetic shiver, since this seems the only transcendentalism left to them. Technique does not mean for him anything very precise. What strikes us is his fine optimistic faith in its powers. Referring to this pristine enthusiasm, he was later to write that he had once worshipped "confusément, mais passionnément, la précision."[2] He has not had time to collect enough information, to study art really intensively; proof, detailed theories are lacking, but the confidence is there, an absolute confidence in the absolute powers of technique. Octave Nadal, writing of Valéry's "mystique spirituelle" during the years 1888 to 1892, shows how Valéry, like many of the symbolist poets, is "en quête de l'unité de l'esprit partout pressentie," a transcendence through poetry and poetic composition.[3] Yet, as early as 1889, we see that this "mystique spirituelle" contains the seeds of the later "mystique intellectuelle" which will displace poetry from its privileged position and make it merely one field of activity for the "esprit universel."

There is some confusion, or at least some ambiguity, in the 1889 article. In its earlier part, Valéry envisages the poet working from something to say or express, something in himself; after which, he supposes, technique will be used by the

---

les jeunes gens nés de 70 à 80 (et d'un certain 'milieu') est à noter. Il y a eu un moment où ce qu'on est convenu d'appeler Beau, Art etc. a failli devenir un culte à mille sectes."

[1] L.Q., p. 46.   [2] *Note et Digression, Vinci,* p. 23.

[3] Introduction (p. 33) to *Paul Valéry–Gustave Fourment. Correspondance* (1887–1933), Paris, Gallimard, 1957.

poet applying certain fundamental laws or principles in order to give this something the most effective expression for the reader. Yet, when he praises Poe, he seems to be considering the poet not as working from something in himself which he wishes to express, but as a craftsman who decides what ought to be said from laws and facts discovered by the study of art and human psychology—working backwards, so to speak, from the reader and using

> une technique entièrement *a posteriori*, établie sur la psychologie de *l'auditeur*, sur la connaissance des diverses notes qu'il s'agit de faire résonner dans l'âme d'autrui.

The quotation begs some obvious questions. Whose desire is concealed in the impersonal "il s'agit de faire?" The poet's? The reader's? If the latter, what reader? The individual something, the something in the poet to be expressed, has been reduced to the concept of the unspecified reader's reaction; this concept, inevitably subjective, is given a spurious objectivity. The confusion of thought indicates that Valéry, still very young, has evidently not yet thought out whether the best kind of poet is trying to express something of himself or whether he is to work *a posteriori* from discoveries in art and psychology, or whether the poet has to do both these things.

What is clear is that, by the time of publication of the *Introduction à la méthode de Léonard de Vinci* (1895) and the *Soirée avec Monsieur Teste* (1896), the uncertainty has disappeared. This is not the occasion to retell in detail Valéry's years of crisis. The *Introduction* and the *Soirée* are the fruits of a certain evolution during which Valéry's "mystique spirituelle" gives place to a "mystique intellectuelle" familiar to every reader of Valéry. The attention of critics has recently been focussed, particularly by Octave Nadal, on the progression from his search for spiritual unity and transcendence through art (as revealed in the years 1888–1892) to the "mystique de l'intellect pur," the realization that all things can be regarded as properties of mind, and the desire to establish a "science autonome du mental."[1] Analogy, as well as being used poetically, can be used scientifically; Valéry's aim will be to discover the means of transposing all phenomena into mathematical symbols or notations; the more numerous the transpositions, the more Valéry will approach the universal unity and complete grasp of the relations between all things. Genius equals "le maximum d'extensions de rapports."[2] Thus Valéry, as he thinks, clarifies certain issues regarding art, science and human knowledge. He develops his passion for knowledge, his attitude to consciousness, his theory of the "esprit universel" and the near-solipsistic attitude outlined in the *Introduction* and confirmed, though rather exaggerated, by other later statements.[3] Valéry grows more and more aware that what interests him is knowledge, and particularly, self-knowledge. He will devote his life to self-knowledge, to the study of "le fonctionnement d'ensemble."[4] The *Soirée* is a delightful, pungent, witty and at the same time serious picture of this cerebral self magnified to the utmost degree, Valéry as he might be if he really, in the future, succeeded in knowing himself completely, if only for "quelques quarts d'heure."[5] The *Introduction*, and especially in its conclusion, indicates that, theoretically at least, all transcendence has now gone out of art for him.

Now, Valéry sees the poet as relying entirely on technique: gone the "rêve," gone the "rêveur affiné." The da Vinci of the *Introduction* is a projection of Valéry's own cerebral self; he is the universal mind who is able to solve all problems of knowledge and technique involving the genius and the external world. Valéry ends his examination of da Vinci with the following generalizations:

Quelques autres minutes de *conscience* peuvent se dépenser à constater qu'il est illusoire de vouloir produire dans l'esprit d'autrui les fantaisies du sien propre. Ce projet est même à

---

[1] Octave Nadal, *op. cit.*, p. 31.   [2] *Ibid.*, p. 37.
[3] Cf. *Propos*, p. 26: "...ayant découvert à l'âge de vingt ans que l'homme est un système fermé quant à la connaissance et aux actes."
[4] *Analecta*, *T.Q. II*, p. 225.   [5] *Teste II, préface*, p. 10.

peu près inintelligible.[1] Ce qu'on appelle une *réalisation* est un *véritable problème de rendement dans lequel n'entre à aucun degré le sens particulier, la clef que chaque auteur attribue à ses matériaux, mais seulement la nature de ces matériaux et l'esprit du public.*[2] Edgar Poe ... a établi clairement, sur la psychologie, sur la probabilité des effets, l'attaque de son lecteur. De ce point de vue, tout déplacement d'élément fait pour être aperçu et jugé dépend de quelques lois générales et d'une appropriation particulière, définie d'avance pour une catégorie prévue d'esprits auxquels ils s'adressent spécialement; et l'œuvre d'art devient une machine destinée à exciter et à combiner les formations individuelles de ces esprits.[3]

We are not told what the "nature de ces matériaux," the "esprit du public" and the "quelques lois générales" are. If Valéry is referring us to those expounded by Poe, he does not explain or comment upon them. He speaks of the "probabilité des effets," not the *infaillibilité* of them, and this calls for explanation if we are not to suspect him of inconsistency.[4] Once again, we note that his confidence in technique is such that he does not take the trouble to give these details. In later life he will do so, as we shall see, but by then he will have modified his views on the relationship between inspiration and technique. In 1895, he cannot give these details, for he has not thought them out.

Tous mes préceptes, trop présents et trop définis, étaient aussi trop universels pour me servir dans aucune circonstance.

---

[1] This is where his solipsistic tendency leads him. We cannot help contrasting this remark with the way in which, throughout the *Introduction*, Valéry succeeds in conveying to us his own "fantaisies".

[2] Our italics.

[3] *Introduction à la méthode de Léonard de Vinci, Vinci*, pp. 116, 117.

[4] In fairness, it should be pointed out that, in a letter to Pierre Louÿs in June 1890, Valéry wrote of the poet as a "sagace algébriste, calculateur infaillible de l'effet à produire" (See *Paul Valéry*: LE CIMETIÈRE MARIN. INTRODUCTION d'*Henri Mondor*, GENÈSE DU POÈME *par* L. J. *Austin*, Grenoble, Roissard, 1954).

Il faut tant d'années pour que les vérités que l'on s'est faites deviennent notre chair même.[1]

The fact that he is not in possession of the details probably explains why his confidence in technique is so unbounded. There is even more of the mystic than of the intellectual in the young Valéry. No wonder that at this stage he more or less gives up the writing of poetry. Literature is "l'art de se jouer de l'âme des autres;" by his own definition, poetry is not now for him the attempt to give expression to something in himself (however deliberately or consciously); the poet gets to know his material (language, poetry), the nature of the public (human psychology in relation to art), and then, like da Vinci, having discovered the "relations . . . entre des choses dont nous échappe la loi de continuité", he can, at will, produce whatever effects he desires to produce in the reader. There is only one thing missing in this ideal scheme: a *desire* on the part of the poet to produce any effect at all. What would be the point? "Le génie est *facile*."[2] "Facil cosa e farsi universale."[3] The young Valéry has more important things to do: he wants to follow up his programme of knowledge and self-knowledge (among other things, to fathom art and psychology, the complete knowledge of which is presumed in the da Vinci and the Monsieur Teste created by him). The art of poetry as defined by Valéry is no longer of any interest from the creative point of view. It demands a "certain sacrifice de l'intellect,"[4] chiefly because he would, if he went on composing poetry, be simply giving to any public for which he wrote what he knows would affect it, playing a rather inferior game which, in theory, he knows he could not lose. The implicit reasoning is somewhat circular. If he were a da Vinci or a Monsieur Teste, he would not trouble himself with poetic composition.[5] So he abandons it. But he is

[1] *Note et Digression, Vinci*, p. 22. This was written in 1919 about his 1894 self.   [2] *La Soirée avec Monsieur Teste, Teste*, p. 37.
[3] *Introduction à la méthode de Léonard de Vinci, Vinci*, p. 71.   [4] *Teste II*, p. 8.
[5] Valéry was to note in 1914: "La théorie dont la littérature est une application, si elle existait, l'application n'en vaudrait plus la peine" (*Cahiers*, tome cinquième, p. 221).

not yet, in fact, a da Vinci or a Monsieur Teste, so he will devote all his time and energy to becoming a universal mind.

Such, in outline, and with only a little simplification, is the theory of the young Valéry concerning inspiration and technique. It is clear that he has not yet formulated clear distinctions between 'total inspiration' and the forms we have called 'intermittent', 'intuitive', 'exalted' and 'personal'; but he rejects them by implication. 'Attributed inspiration' would presumably, it is true, have been accepted by him. But the other five forms he would have rejected: his theory allows them to be completely dispensed with.

But is his theory convincing? Let us consider the first of the two conceptions of creation implicit in the *Technique littéraire* article, according to which the poet has something in himself, impression, dream or thought, which he must communicate by controlled technique. Whilst surely nearer the truth than the other, the theory that works backwards, even this conception seems mechanistic, too simple and unsatisfactory. Valéry does not examine how impression, dream or thought originate. There is no mention of any possible dynamism behind them, no mention of the fact that the initial impetus may be accompanied by emotion or excitement which are commonly envisaged as attributes of inspiration. It may be conceded that poetry is certainly the communication of something, and that accordingly it is sound to claim that the poet is concerned with an audience, so that the more knowledge he has of this audience and of the nature of his art, the better. But it is surely not simply a question, in poetic creation, of the poet's having something clearly formed in his mind, even something so vague as a dream, and then transferring it to a reader by the technique of language. The truth surely is (and the mature Valéry certainly subscribed to this view) that the poet is concerned with clarifying and making enjoyably articulate for himself and the reader something within him which does not exist as poetry until the poem is composed. Given the nature of language and poetic creation, the poet is, to a certain extent, discovering what he has to say, or rather, what he can say, as he composes the poem. The poem is a kind of compromise between what the poet wanted to say initially (and this phrase 'what the poet wanted to say' is perhaps too rational and explicit to describe what for many poets is vague and more anticipation than exact intention at this stage), what he finds to say, and all the new things to express which occur to him as he actually composes the poem. All these aspects of poetic creation will indeed be admirably brought out by the mature Valéry. Louis MacNeice writes of that "dialect of purification" whereby a poem is produced,

> a poem which is neither the experience nor the memory, nor an abstract dance of words, but a new life composite of all three.[1]

In this respect, then, poetry can be considered as a kind of knowledge, of self-knowledge particularly, only to be found during the struggle to compose. Valéry in his youth does not show much awareness of these aspects of poetic creation and of this kind of self-knowledge. He is obsessed with the notion of art as communication, and therefore with the fact that, though the poet may be able to make the reader react as he wishes by his all-conquering technique, he is nevertheless, because he indulges in poetic composition, a slave to the reader and to language:

> chaque esprit qu'on trouve puissant, commence par la faute qui le fait connaître. En échange du pourboire public, il donne le temps qu'il faut pour se rendre perceptible, l'énergie dissipée à se transmettre et à préparer la satisfaction étrangère.[2]

We are thus led on to the second theory of poetry revealed with some uncertainty in the *Technique littéraire* article and unequivocally expounded towards the end of the *Introduction à la méthode de Léonard de Vinci*, the theory according to which

---

[1] C. Day Lewis, *The Poetic Image*, London, Jonathan Cape, 1947, p. 86.
[2] *La Soirée avec Monsieur Teste, Teste*, pp. 24, 25.

the poet works backwards from the reader. This stands condemned on two counts. Firstly, it is a partial view of poetic
creation, neglecting the personal contribution which the poet
can, must, make (i.e. 'personal inspiration'; and this is not to
mention the importance of 'intermittent', 'intuitive' and
'exalted inspiration'). Valéry is at least consistent: having
defined the work of art as "une machine destinée à exciter et à
combiner les formations individuelles de ces esprits" (the
public), he rejects such an activity as beneath him, as time-
wasting when he has more important things to do. His initial
definition of art is faulty, incomplete. Secondly, it stands
condemned by the very inadequacy of its presentation. Not
only is art ill defined, but no details are given of the nature of
human psychology on which the success of the triumphant
technique is supposed to depend. The fact is that, at this stage
of his career, he has no adequate theory of language and no
adequate conception of poetic creation such as he will have in
later years. Few would question the value of technique, but how
many would subscribe to the exaggerated thesis put forward
by Valéry in his youth?

*

Nothing is more significant than the detached humour with
which Valéry, in 1919, in the *Note et Digression* which he wrote
for his *Introduction à la méthode de Léonard de Vinci*, looks back,
not without sympathy despite the detachment, at the ideas and
difficulties which he had had in 1894, about the time of
composition of the *Introduction*. He excuses himself, so to speak,
but does not really explain enough for our purposes. We are
still left wondering why he should have had this absolute faith
in the powers of technique and why therefore he believed, if
only for a short time, that poetry can be composed without any
trace of inspiration. The influence of Poe and Mallarmé, and
the part it played in Valéry's abandonment of poetry and the
development of his programme of knowledge and self-
knowledge, has been clearly indicated by Valéry himself and
often discussed by his critics. Less attention has been paid to an

influence probably no less potent: that of contemporary scientific thought.[1]

The last three decades of the nineteenth century were an age in which, as the rift between philosophy and science widened, it was becoming evident that there was more than one reality, depending on the viewpoint of the observer. The scientist was cautious of claiming to interpret or explain phenomena: on the one hand, there was reality with its multiple facets, on the other, the man who sought to understand this reality. His understanding was necessarily subjective, but hope lay in his attempt to capture the manifold aspects of this reality. In fact, reality as such had no meaning: it is we who supply the meaning. The upshot of these tendencies of enlightened positivism was that the scientist avoided any metaphysical claims for his discoveries (similarly, Valéry had rejected philosophy, metaphysics, any form of 'absolute' in the normal sense): he sought a limited goal, continuity, by establishing relationships between phenomena.

Henri Poincaré probably played a decisive rôle in causing Valéry to shift his attention "from 'objects in themselves' to the 'relationships existing between objects', in which alone is any meaning to be found."[2] Thanks to his purely personal pre-

---

[1] Part of our examination of the importance for Valéry of contemporary scientific thought, both here and later in the chapter, has appeared in an article, *The Sonnet* LE VIN PERDU *of Paul Valéry*, French Studies, Vol. X, No. 1, January 1956. Until the autumn of 1960, the fullest estimate of Valéry's links with scientific thought (and particularly with Poincaré) had been made by F. E. Sutcliffe, *La Pensée de Paul Valéry. Essai*, Paris, Nizet, 1955. The present study had gone to press before the appearance of Judith Robinson's excellent and comprehensive article on *Language, Physics and Mathematics in Valéry's Cahiers*, Modern Language Review, Vol. LV, No. 4, October 1960.

[2] R. S. Jones, *Poincaré and Valéry; a note on the 'symbol' in science and art*, in *Modern Language Review*, vol. XLII, no. 4, October 1947, p. 487. The author supports his contention with the following quotation from Poincaré's *La Valeur de la Science* (pp. 265, 266 and 271): "Maintenant qu'est-ce que la science?... c'est avant tout une classification... un système de relations. Or... c'est dans les relations seulement que l'objectivité doit être cherchée... C'est ce lien, et ce lien seul qui est objet en eux [i.e. in external objects], et ce lien c'est un rapport. Donc quand nous demandons quelle est la valeur

occupations (his cult of consciousness, together with his reaction against love and poetry, "less choses vagues" generally), thanks to the influence of Mallarmé's formalism, Valéry was already by the early 1890s well along the road of 'relations' as opposed to 'objects in themselves'. Marked similarities of attitude can be discovered between the views of Poincaré and Valéry on intellectual creation, both poetic and scientific.[1] Valéry writes in 1919:

> Toutes choses se substituent,—ne serait-ce pas la définition des *choses*?[2]

and, in 1944, looking back to his youth:

> Il y eut un temps où je voyais. Je voyais ou voulais voir les figures de relations entre les choses, et non les choses. Les *choses* me faisaient sourire de pitié. Ceux qui s'y arrêtaient ne m'étaient que des idolâtres. Je *savais* que l'essentiel était *figure*. Et c'était une sorte de mysticisme, puisque c'était faire dépendre le monde sensible aux yeux, d'un monde sensible à l'esprit et réservé, supposant révélation, initiation, etc.[3]

The young Valéry is interested in the "esprit universel," da Vinci or Napoleon, whose supreme secret

> est et ne peut être que dans les relations qu'ils trouvèrent, —qu'ils furent forcés de trouver,—*entre des choses dont nous échappe la loi de continuité.*[4]

Valéry is drawn by the rigour and the universality of mathematics and of positivistic science generally towards the end of the nineteenth century. His da Vinci of the *Introduction*, his Monsieur Teste, are animated by a central belief in the *continu*; his attitude before 1900, and even long after that date, like that

---

objective de la science, cela ne veut, pas dire: la science nous fait-elle connaître la véritable nature des choses? mais cela veut dire; nous fait-elle connaître les véritables rapports des choses?... En résumé, la seule réalité objective, ce sont les rapports d'où résulte l'harmonie universelle."

[1] See F. E. Sutcliffe, *op. cit.*, pp. 76–91.
[2] *Note et Digression, Vinci*, p. 47.   [3] *Propos*, p. 53.
[4] *Introduction à la méthode de Léonard de Vinci, Vinci*, p. 70.

of Poincaré, rests on the postulate that we cannot yet explain all the relations between all phenomena, but that we shall be able to do so eventually. The da Vinci of the *Introduction* believes that our inability to see everything minutely and clearly is due merely to the infirmity of our senses; such was Clerk Maxwell's point of view, as exemplified by his imaginary demon who could perform various fantastic tasks beyond the powers of ordinary men. The function of the universal mind is to transform *discontinu* into *continu*, and there is a tacit assumption that if this process can be continued, all the elements which do not fit in with what we already know, all the *discontinu*, past, present or future, will be transformed into *continu*. Maxwell's demon is essentially the same monster as Valéry's da Vinci—a projection to the infinite of their positivistic belief in *rapports* and the possibility of explaining the relationships between everything.[1] Maxwell's demon and Valéry's da Vinci (or Teste) are what Poincaré, Maxwell and Valéry wanted to be, hoped to be—the universal mind. This Maxwell-Poincaré-Valéry relationship becomes all the more understandable if we remember that Poincaré, naturally, was well acquainted with the work of Maxwell,[2] and Valéry acquainted with the work of both Poincaré and Maxwell.[3]

[1] Cf. F. E. Sutcliffe, *op. cit.*, p. 106: "Nous avons assez longuement parlé de la notion de continu telle qu'elle apparaît dans les premiers essais de Valéry, et nous en avons indiqué les rapports avec la notion mathématique de continuité. Rappelons que celle-ci postule le pouvoir de l'esprit de s'asservir l'hétérogène, de dépasser le discontinu. L'esprit crée donc le continu en conjuguant des rapports, en formulant des lois scientifiques." And also, p. 111: "Le caractère essentiel du réel c'est le continu et toute discontinuité n'est qu'une vue de l'esprit, une convention introduite par l'esprit pour mieux se permettre de cerner le réel."

[2] Cf. Poincaré's work, *La théorie de Maxwell et les oscillations herziennes*, 1899.

[3] For Valéry's knowledge of Poincaré, see *Introduction à la méthode de Léonard de Vinci*, *Vinci*, p. 74, footnote, and the information given to Maurice Bémol by Valéry's son, Claude, and by Julien Monod, p. 213 of Bémol's thesis, *Paul Valéry*, Paris, Les Belles Lettres, 1949. For Valéry's knowledge of Clerk Maxwell, cf. the references to Maxwell in the *Introduction*, *Vinci*, pp. 113, 114.

So we see how Valéry came to transfer his interests and hopes from poetic creation to this positivistic ideal of universal knowledge. With a youthful enthusiasm and impatience which he later acknowledged in the *Note et Digression* of 1919, he fathoms, as he thinks, "le problème littéraire" in the way we have seen, and more or less abandons poetic composition:

> Lorsque j'ai commencé de fréquenter Mallarmé en personne,[1] la littérature ne m'était presque plus de rien. Lire et écrire me pesaient... La conscience de moi-même pour elle-même, l'éclaircissement de cette attention, et le souci de me dessiner nettement mon existence ne me quittaient guère. Ce mal secret éloigne des Lettres, desquelles cependant il tient son origine.[2]

Poe and Mallarmé had, in a sense, led him in the same direction as Poincaré. He is strong in his belief that there is

> une sorte de contraste entre l'exercice de la littérature et la poursuite d'une certaine rigueur et d'une entière sincérité de la pensée.[3]

Science and a certain ideal of self-knowledge can, he now discovers, lead to transcendence. His new ideal gives him absolute faith in the absolute powers of technique, hence the enthusiasm and vigour of his pronouncements against inspiration. He expresses this faith in the *Introduction* and the *Soirée* as if he actually had at his disposal a certain mastery of the positivistic programme outlined above, as if he had actually realized his ideal of universal knowledge. The language he uses in 1919 to describe his youthful self of 1894 is significant:

> Je *sentais*[4] que ce maître de ses moyens [i.e. Léonard de Vinci], ce possesseur du dessin, des images, du calcul avait trouvé

---

[1] In October 1891.

[2] This point in the last sentence is echoed by E. Noulet (*Paul Valéry*, Bruxelles, Editions de l'oiseau bleu, 1927) and by Octave Nadal in his introduction to the Valéry-Fourment correspondence.

[3] *Dernière Visite à Mallarmé*, Mall., pp. 23, 24.   [4] Our italics.

l'attitude centrale à partir de laquelle les entreprises de la connaissance et les opérations de l'art sont également possibles; les échanges heureux entre l'analyse et les actes, singulièrement probables; pensée merveilleusement excitante.[1]

The faith in the power of intellect is the guiding principle with which he enters his so-called years of silence, when his main object will be at first to achieve what it pleased him to imagine that da Vinci had achieved—"le développement de la conscience pour les fins de la connaissance,"[2] what Teste was supposed to have achieved—"se figurer aussi simplement, aussi nettement que possible, [son] propre fonctionnement d'ensemble."[3]

*

By Valéry's *maturity*, we understand his thought and preoccupations as they are revealed by his publications from 1918 to his death in 1945. It is during this period that we find the main body of his writings, especially on poetry. After 1918, Valéry sometimes worked on a selection of notes from his *cahiers* and published it.[4] Now that the notebooks for the so-called years of silence have been published, it is confirmed that the essentially analytical work of those years provided the foundation for Valéry's later, published, views. The years 1896–1917 mark for our present purposes a period of transition of which at least the last dozen years can be seen as preparing or merging into Valéry's maturity.

Let us first set down some general conclusions about the difference in Valéry's thought between youth and maturity. His "mystique intellectuelle" as formulated in his youth remains the basis of his attitude to our problem in that the desire for universal knowledge and utter lucidity naturally prejudices him

---

[1] *Note et Digression, Vinci*, p. 15.
[2] *Une Vue de Descartes, Var. V*, p. 250.   [3] *Analecta, T.Q. II*, p. 225.
[4] Cf. the *Avis au lecteur*, p. 7 of *Mélange*: "Il n'est pas de livre dont le titre soit plus vrai que celui-ci. Le désordre qui 'règne' (comme on dit) dans *Mélange* s'étend à la chronologie. Telle chose a été écrite il y a près de cinquante ans. Telle autre est d'avant-hier!"

against inspiration and in favour of technique. But it is clear that his position has changed since 1896. The years 1896 to 1913 or even 1917 did not bring the realization of the programme implicit in the "mystique intellectuelle" of his youth. He writes, for instance, as early as 1906:

> Heureusement n'ai-je jamais cru à la cité future, et je ne puis même plus croire à cet Eden de lucidité, à cette extrémité de pureté ni à cet ut de tête logique où jadis je sentais Narcisse et naguère mon bon M. Teste.[1]

Valéry's dream of universal knowledge reminds us of the similarly impossible ideals of Mallarmé and Rimbaud. He grew more and more keenly aware that, by the very nature of his quest for precision, universal knowledge and self-knowledge, *reality* was always in the last analysis unknowable and beyond his grasp. For "la conscience"—that analytical awareness, particularly of self, which is the prerogative of intellect and which remained the guiding factor of his life—is a "refus indéfini d'être quoi que ce soit;"[2] by its very nature, it implies the separation of the observer and the observed.[3] Discouraging is a mild word to describe the awful complexity which acute 'awareness'[4] brings to all research of the type Valéry undertakes.

---

[1] *L.Q.*, p. 73.

[2] The word *conscience* rarely means for Valéry "la conscience (genre moral)" (*Cahiers, tome sixième*, p. 416). It means consciousness and often, as well, consciousness of self (like "le moi pur" and "la conscience de la conscience"); it implies an almost inhuman detachment. He explains in *Cahiers, tome deuxième*, p. 120 that he means "conscience au sens de Poe, c à d. l'idée que telle idée est une idée." For Valéry, "la conscience est l'extérieur de toute chose—l'éternel dehors" (*Cahiers, tome troisième*, p. 740).

[3] Cf. *Cahiers, tome sixième*, p. 898: "ns ne pouvons parler des choses ou les penser que par ignorance—c à d. qu'en les rendant bien distinctes de nous, bien étrangères à nous.

"En prendre connaissance, c'est s'en séparer—Les voir nettement c'est les prévoir, c'est ne pas y être.

"De là cette grande opposition entre la connaissance et l'être..."

[4] This word will be used throughout this study to convey what Valéry means by "le moi pur," "la conscience de la conscience" and, often, "la conscience."

He notes in *Analecta* (1926) that

pour une certaine division trop fine ou attention trop poussée, les *choses* perdent leur *sens*. On dépasse un certain 'optimum' de la compréhension, ou de la relation possible entre l'homme et ses propriétés: ... On voit, mais on a perdu ses notions à la porte. Ce qu'on voit est indubitable et inconcevable. La partie et le tout ne communiquent plus.[1]

How much more discouraging when the very notion of knowing reality crumbles if the reality can be known only at arm's length! 'Awareness' fragments reality into a greater and greater number of elements, too complex to be embraced by one mind and, in any case, known only in that they are different and distinct from that mind. It is unlikely that this consideration occurred to Valéry for the first time in his maturity. The point is that the painful awareness of the dilemma works cumulatively as he lives with and experiences it more and more deeply. Thus one reads in the *Extraits du Log-book de M. Teste*:

Il y a des personnages qui sentent que leurs sens les séparent du réel, de l'être. Ce sens en eux *infecte* leurs autres sens.
Ce que je vois m'aveugle. Ce que j'entends m'assourdit. Ce en quoi je sais, cela me rend ignorant. J'ignore en tant et pour autant que je sais. Cette illumination devant moi est un bandeau et recouvre ou une nuit ou une lumière plus ...
Plus quoi? Ici le cercle se ferme, de cet étrange renversement: la connaissance, comme un nuage sur l'être; le monde brillant, comme taie et opacité.
Otez toute chose que j'y voie.[2]

The realization of this dilemma is acute at least as early as 1913, since the last quotation is in the *cahier* for that year. It is interesting to note how the realization is linked with his attitude towards science in so far as science is the attempt to formulate reality or notions about reality. It would be imprudent to talk of the *influence* of scientific thought on Valéry in

[1] *Analecta*, T.Q. II, p. 274.
[2] *Extraits du log-book de Monsieur Teste*, *Teste*, p. 71.

this context, for it might just as well be a question of his own experience often influencing his attitude to science: he would naturally tend to dwell on those aspects of modern scientific thought which fit in with his own attitude. Yet there were certain objective facts in scientific thought in the early part of this century which may well have confirmed an attitude already present in Valéry by about 1910.

By 1920, and even more by 1930, scientific thought had undergone profound change since the end of the previous century. Einstein's theory of relativity, J. J. Thomson's discovery of the electron, Max Planck's quantum theory are specific instances of the discoveries and theories which were to revolutionize science. In the early part of the twentieth century, with the increasing tempo of the development of atomic physics (witness, from 1924 onwards, the work of Louis de Broglie, developed by Schrödinger and Heisenberg, which led to the modification of the original quantum theory and the view that electrons and protons are themselves to be considered as wave motion), an entirely new conception of reality was to be developed. *Le continu* gave way to *le discontinu* : the scientist could not now cherish so easily the hope that all phenomena, that the relationships between phenomena, could be co-ordinated and made clear. Man was bewildered by the heterogeneity of the phenomena revealed by modern science.

From 1920 onwards, Valéry stresses *le discontinu* more and more, stating time and time again that it now seems impossible to envisage a definite corpus of knowledge, because all so-called knowledge is only a means to an end, which is verifiable action. Thus, in *Au Sujet d'Eureka* (1924), he shows that it is now no longer possible to distinguish between matter and energy. He also affirms that

> le déterminisme se perd dans ces systèmes inextricables à milliards de variables, où l'œil de l'esprit ne peut plus suivre les lois et s'arrêter sur quelque chose qui se conserve. Quand la discontinuité devient la règle, l'imagination qui jadis s'employait à achever la vérité que les perceptions avaient

fait soupçonner et les raisonnements tissue, se doit déclarer impuissante.[1]

Similarly, in 1934, he writes to Henri Bergson:

Je ne saurais maintenant—ni sans doute jamais, entrer dans le détail de cette discussion [la grande affaire de la Relativité], mais je me permets cette remarque. La Physique qui, depuis 30 ans, ne cesse de battre ses cartes et de nous jeter sur le tapis les combinaisons les plus surprenantes des variables de son jeu, nous prie à présent de considérer que dans l'intime de l'atome, rien ne va plus comme à l'extérieur. Il semble que ni le temps ni l'espace, ni les positions, ni la succession elle-même—et ni les images ni les repères n'ont plus de sens, dans les coulisses de la nature.[2]

"L'imagination... se doit déclarer impuissante." How much autobiography dare one read into such sentences? Let there be no misunderstanding here. Valéry will always make an idol of intellect and for the Valéry of 1945 as well as for the Valéry of 1896 it may be fairly said that

le but constant de l'investigation reste le pays mental, et l'expression de ce dernier dans une langue exacte.[3]

He clung tenaciously to his cult of intellect right to the end, despite certain effects of it in the modern world which he clearly and eloquently deplored.[4] Yet, like the scientists, he seems to abandon the hope of a complete formulation, a definitive correlation of all phenomena, that is, for him, all mental phenomena, the

formes symboliques organisées en séries continues, parfaite-ment liées, lisibles et maniables au regard de l'esprit.[5]

---

[1] *Au sujet d'Eureka*, in *Variété*, p. 125, quoted by F. E. Sutcliffe, *op. cit.*, p. 128.

[2] L.Q., pp. 220, 221.

[3] Octave Nadal in his introduction to the Valéry-Fourment correspond-ence, p. 37.

[4] Cf. F. E. Sutcliffe, *op. cit.*   [5] Octave Nadal, *op. cit.*, p. 33.

He still judges everything by the light of his "moi pur," but no longer with the same enthusiasm and hope that inspired him in 1896. The preoccupations remain, and will always remain, largely the same, but the whole tone and attitude have changed since his youth: witness the ultra-detached, wry humour of his description of himself in his mature years:

> Le serpent se mange la queue. Mais, ce n'est qu'après un long temps de mastication qu'il reconnaît le gout du serpent. Il s'arrête alors. Mais, au bout d'un autre temps, n'ayant rien d'autre à manger, il s'y remet. Il arrive alors à avoir sa tête dans sa gueule. C'est ce qu'il appelle "une théorie de la Connaissance."[1]

"Il n'a jamais été tenté de s'accorder dialectiquement,"[2] in Jean Hytier's happy phrase; this is true of the mature Valéry, the Valéry revealed by the bulk of his publications, but it is not true of the universal mind he had hoped to become in the last decade of the nineteenth century. For the high ambition of those confident days, he later feels something like nostalgia:

> Sans doute n'est-il pas impossible que j'aie quelquefois imaginé 'l'univers des pensées' comme un système fermé, analogue à l'univers des sons et tenté d'en rechercher les propriétés et virtualités *intrinsèques*, et je vous avoue que je crois que c'est là une vue des plus relevées . . . Je sais bien que je pouvais tout comme un autre, abuser des mots et sembler dépasser les pouvoirs de l'intellect, jouer de la sensibilité par des figures et des combinaisons abstraites qui donnent beaucoup d'espoir aux gens. Mais je n'appelle vérité que ce qui est vérifiable.[3]

In the last sentence, we have the voice of the mature Valéry who has not only found his ideal impossible to realize, but who,

---

[1] *P.V.V.*, p. 276.

[2] Jean Hytier, *La Poétique de Valéry*, Paris, Colin, 1953, p. 247.

[3] Letter from Valéry to Edmond Buchet in the latter's book, *Ecrivains intelligents du vingtième siècle*, Paris, Corréa, 1945, pp. 163 and 167.

perhaps to some extent under the influence of modern science, has also learnt to suspect any attempt to say the last word.

Il y a quelque ridicule aujourd'hui à prétendre 'expliquer'. La conception d'un système semble aussi fausse que celle d'un outil universel.[1]

This modification of his early viewpoint naturally influenced his views on the question of inspiration and technique, leading him to make less extravagant claims for technique. We shall see this more clearly as we examine the mature Valéry's views in detail.

Another factor which undoubtedly reinforced this tendency to less extravagant claims for technique was his full return to poetic creation from 1913 onwards. While composing *La Jeune Parque* and the poems of *Charmes*, he was able to put what theories he had formed to the test of practice in a much more comprehensive manner than he had been able to do since the 1890s. Despite his constant preference for technique, for controlled poetic creation, Valéry was too honest not to admit, however guarded his language, that inspiration has an important, if limited, part to play in the poetic act. He was also more able to distinguish and analyse the different implications of the concept of inspiration, and to speak more clearly of the various stages in poetic creation.

This modification of his early views was not conceded without a struggle. He never entirely abandons his old dream and, as we have already said, he remains until his death suspicious of writing said to be inspired. But the holes in the ancient dream's fabric are made all the more apparent by the very way in which he frequently attacks inspiration. The Valéry who became famous in the 1920s seems to have scandalized many people by certain trenchant formulae stressing the conscious aspect of the poetic act and ridiculing the inspirational aspect. Thus, on many occasions, he is concerned to discuss, not so much whether inspiration exists, as whether it can, alone,

---

[1] *P.V.V.*, p. 269.

create a work of art in its entirety.[1] In other words, many of his most striking formulae attacking inspiration are directed against 'total inspiration'. Opposing the idea of the supernatural origin of inspiration as much as the idea that inspiration can dictate a whole poem, he has no difficulty in scoring his point. If the notion of inspiration which he is attacking were sound, the inspired poet could write in any language, not just his own, he would be utterly at the command of an external force and could be compared to "une sorte d'urne en laquelle des millions de billes sont agitées" or to a "*table tournante* dans laquelle un *esprit* se loge" or to a recording apparatus, or to a medium.[2] Valéry's sarcasm easily dismissed so naïve a conception of inspiration:

> Un jour, quelqu'un m'apprit que le lyrisme est enthousiasme, et que les odes des grands lyriques furent écrites sans retour, à la vitesse de la voix du délire et du vent de l'esprit soufflant en tempête ... Je lui répondis qu'il était tout à fait dans le vrai; mais que ce n'était pas là un privilège de la poésie et que tout le monde savait que pour construire une locomotive, il est indispensable que le constructeur prenne l'allure de 80 milles à l'heure pour exécuter son travail.[3]

Blake, as we have seen, sought to persuade his readers that he wrote under the compulsion of 'total inspiration'; Shelley left certain of his poems unfinished, on the pretext that inspiration had deserted him. It is doubtful, however, whether even the romantic poets in general really believed in 'total inspiration': their practice, at least, too often makes such a belief on their part incredible. Even though some would scarcely think them worth making, let Valéry be granted his points: inspiration cannot dictate a whole poem, inspiration is not of supernatural origin. This constant tendency to depreciate inspiration is to be expected, given his aims and preoccupations.

---

[1] Cf. Jean Hytier, *op. cit.*, p. 128.
[2] *Propos sur la poésie*, *Conf.*, pp. 81, 82.
[3] *Poésie et pensée abstraite*, *Var. V*, p. 159.

L'idée d'inspiration, si l'on se tient à cette image naïve d'un souffle étranger, ou d'une âme toute puissante, substituée tout à coup, pour un temps, à la nôtre, peut suffire à la mythologie ordinaire des choses de l'esprit. Presque tous les poètes s'en contentent[?]. Bien plutôt, ils n'en veulent point souffrir d'autre. Mais je ne puis arriver à comprendre que l'on ne cherche pas à descendre dans soi-même le plus profondément qu'il soit possible. Il paraît qu'on risque son salut à tenter d'en explorer les Enfers. Mais qu'importe ce salut? Trouvera-t-on pas *autre chose*?[1]

This "autre chose" is, of course, precise knowledge of the events in poetic creation, any information which can be incorporated into Valéry's programme of universal knowledge.

But the fact is that he admits the existence of inspiration for others and for himself on many occasions and in tones varying from reluctant concession to ecstatic approval. It is true that inspiration can give only fragments of good poetry which have to be consciously worked together with other fragments not so inspired. In a famous statement by Valéry, it appears that one criterion of good verse is the quality of that poetry which comes with inspiration, and that technique consists in using all one's efforts to equal the excellence of such inspiration. The distance is great from the Valéry of 1895 or 1896 to the Valéry who thus writes:

Les dieux gracieusement nous donnent *pour rien* tel premier vers; mais c'est à nous de façonner le second, qui doit consonner avec l'autre, et ne pas être indigne de son aîné surnaturel. Ce n'est pas trop de toutes les ressources de l'expérience et de l'esprit pour le rendre comparable au vers qui fut un don.[2]

Empiricism tends to be the keynote of the older Valéry's thought, and this is true of his thought about poetic composition. The ambition, fired by his reading of Poe, to discover an

---

[1] L.Q., p. 160.   [2] *Au sujet d'Adonis, Var. 1948*, p. 73.

all-embracing technique was never realized. He wrote in his maturity:

> Il m'est arrivé d'envisager d'une façon tout à fait théorique la construction d'un ouvrage littéraire, une œuvre montée de toutes pièces, étudiée dans ses moindres parties comme on étudie une machine très complexe. Je ne l'ai jamais mise en chantier.[1]

His writings on poetry constitute an immense accumulation of detailed observations which are more or less connected but not always completely or satisfactorily. He is not easily pinned down. His views are not always consistent with each other; he boasted that "il y a de la pauvreté d'esprit à être toujours d'accord avec soi-même,"[2] and in any given period of his life his statements concerning our problem can vary considerably. The difficulties he raises are often great but, though he does not and cannot solve them all, the light he sheds is preferable to the semi-darkness which prevailed before. It is clear enough that he had to reject 'total inspiration'. His detailed analyses of the five other forms of inspiration, not clarified before his mature years, will occupy our attention in the subsequent chapters.

[1] *La Création artistique, Vues,* p. 308.
[2] *Lettre-Préface* in Emile Rideau, *Introduction à la pensée de Paul Valéry,* Paris, Desclée de Brouwer, 1944, p. 3.

CHAPTER II

MIND AND BODY

VALERY was a poet and aesthetician; he was also in some measure, and inevitably, a psychologist when he studied artistic creation. It will greatly help our understanding of his conception of inspiration and technique and his psychology of the poet and reader if we know something of his views on what he called the human "fonctionnement d'ensemble."[1] "Internité" is another term which he once used which seems to indicate how any one part of the "fonctionnement d'ensemble" is essentially linked with all the others.[2] He consigned to his notebooks a

quantité absurde de notes et d'ébauches de systèmes (se rattachant à une représentation du fonctionnement humain).[3]

In a letter to Jean de Latour, he confided that

c'est ... sur des idées physiologiques, disons fonctionnelles, qu' [il avait], depuis quarante ans, médité le plus. Ces réflexions remplissent des volumes de notes.[4]

Our concern here will be with these views only in so far as they relate to our problem. They will be taken mainly from his published notes and particularly from some of the *cours de poétique* which he gave at the *Collège de France* from 1937 almost until his death in 1945. In our attempt to present a brief and coherent account of his views we shall inevitably schematize and be tempted to refer to his *theories*. It is therefore useful to recall that, for his part, he usually refused to form permanent theories. He lived or said he lived in "l'éternellement provisoire."[5] In the light of his sole "invariant,"[6] 'awareness', he reserved the right to change or modify any judgement previous-

---

[1] *Analecta, T.Q. II*, p. 225.　　[2] *L.Q.*, p. 20.　　[3] *Ibid.*, p. 225.
[4] Jean de Latour, *Examen de Valéry*, p. 7.　　[5] *L.Q.*, p. 245.
[6] *Note et Digression, Vinci*, p. 52.

ly formed. But, in his maturer years, he seems to have claimed this right perhaps more than he used it. He has the advantage over us, in that his genius can always smile and point scornfully at our attempts to systematize mere glimpses and suggestions put forward with wit, humour and varying degrees of diffidence, feigned or authentic. Our justification for speaking of *theories* is that this attitude had perhaps at times something of the pose in it. Moreover, reading his works and those *cours de poétique* that survive, we can find certain theories or at least the emergence of quasi-theories—"ébauches de systèmes," to use his own phrase[1]—in the very frequency of certain suggestions.

What might be called Valéry's point of departure in this field was inevitably more striking earlier in this century than it appears now. Thanks to his cult of 'awareness', analysis and self-control, he realized how arbitrary and unreal were some of the accepted classifications and groupings in human psychology. He said that

> plus une conscience est 'consciente', plus *son* personnage, plus *ses* opinions, *ses* actes, *ses* caractéristiques, *ses* sentiments, lui paraissent *étranges*,—étrangers. Elle tendrait donc à disposer de ce qu'elle a de plus propre comme de choses extérieures et accidentelles.[2]

The classifications *character* and *personality* do not withstand a serious examination,[3] nor likewise any other concept similar to these two, such as *soul* and *mind* or *spirit*.

> Le Moi n'est relativement précis qu'en tant qu'il est une notation d'usage externe . . . la notation *moi* ne désigne rien de déterminé que dans la circonstance et par elle; et s'il demeure quelque chose, ce n'est que la notion pure de présence, de la capacité d'une infinité de modifications. Finalement, *ego* se réduit à *quoi que ce soit*.[4]

---

[1] Cf. p. 35, note 3.   [2] *Choses tues, T.Q. I,* p. 63.
[3] *Analecta, T.Q. II,* p. 263.   [4] *Fluctuations sur la liberté, Regards,* p. 80.

The word which Valéry used most to describe our internal activities was "sensibilité." The influence of sensibility, as he understands the word, is all-powerful.[1] According to him, man is distinguishable from the animal and greater than it because he is prone to dwell on perceptions that are of no immediate practical value, since they result in ideas, images, impulsions which find no external outlet. We receive more sensations and are capable of more potential actions than we need to live a practical life devoted to the satisfaction of our basic vital wants.[2] Sensibility denotes all this indivisible internal activity, which seems almost a world in itself. The function of all the arts, Valéry thinks, is to feed this sensibility, this "puissance cachée qui fait toutes les fables." [3]

What are the characteristics of sensibility? It is intense, variable and discontinuous.[4] Its activity is virtually unceasing.[5] This last trait is linked with another—important in Valéry's aesthetic—its "caractère récepto-émetteur." [6] It abhors a vacuum: [7]

Elle est productrice et s'oppose à l'absence de suffisantes excitations, réagit contre leur rareté. Toutes les fois où surgit une certaine durée vide de sensations particulières, naît en

---

[1] Cf. *Histoires brisées*, p. 126: "Les vrais dieux sont les forces ou puissances de la sensibilité," and *Suite, T.Q. II*, p. 311: "Le plus grand problème, l'unique, est celui de la sensibilité."

[2] *Cours de poétique* of 17 December 1937.

[3] *Cours de poétique* of 11 February 1938.

[4] *Cours de poétique* of 18 December 1937.

[5] *L'Idée fixe*, p. 101: "Un homme à l'état non sollicité est à l'état néant." *Variations sur une pensée, Var. II*, p. 57: "Sensibilité... ne connaît point d'équilibre. On pourrait même la définir comme une fonction dont le rôle est de rompre dans les vivants tout équilibre de leurs puissances."

[6] *Cours de poétique* of 17 December 1937, in *Yggdrasill*, 25 January 1938. We shall refer from time to time to the reports of the first year's lectures on poetics made by Georges le Breton in *Yggdrasill*. These accounts are useful in that they save us from quoting too much and too often from Madame Valéry's unpublished typescripts.

[7] See *Léonard et les philosophes, Vinci*, p. 131, and also *cours de poétique* of 17 December 1937, in *Yggdrasill* of 25 January 1938.

nous une émission qui tend à remplir cette vacance. Une production d'énergie spéciale en nous demande à s'employer.[1]

Sensibility denotes for Valéry the composite internal state of mind and body. Many times, particularly in the *cours de poétique*, when he tries to explain what he means by the word, he despairs:

> Si le mot 'mystère' a un sens, je ne lui vois de plus juste emploi que de qualifier cette substance de tout, la sensibilité.[2]

He refers in *Mélange* to

> ces régions de l'être où la sensibilité à l'état brut, et les étranges énergies dont elle dispose sont inaccessibles,—réalité pure. Là se chargent et se déchargent nos capacités de volupté et de douleur. Ni doutes, ni discussions dans ce domaine. Il est impénétrable aux raisons, qui ne sont que parole, aux évidences qui ne sont que lumière froide. La conscience même, et même une connaissance précise du mécanisme de ce mal, ne peuvent rien contre lui . . .[3]

This is the mature Valéry speaking, the Valéry who has come to recognize that technique, the prerogative of intellect, cannot by any means always control or do without inspiration, the prerogative of sensibility. Indeed, he seems to envisage the "fonctionnement d'ensemble" as a tug-of-war between the intellect and sensibility:

> la sensibilité est tout, moins ce que nous avons pu lui soustraire: alors nous sommes dans l'état d'intellectualité pure.[4]

We have thus an adumbration of the familiar dichotomies intellect-sensibility, consciousness-unconsciousness, technique-inspiration. Everything in the domain of intellect is opposed to sensibility—formal logic, for instance, and especially science as

---

[1] *Cours de poétique* of 17 December 1937, in *Yggdrasill* of 25 January 1938.
[2] *Au sujet de Berthe Morisot, Vues*, p. 240.   [3] *Mélange*, p. 112.
[4] *Cours de poétique* of 8 January 1938, in *Yggdrasill* of 25 January 1938.

we know it now.[1] But Valéry warns us that intellect and
sensibility are not clearly separate entities. He therefore at times
speaks of "sensibilité généralisée,"[2] a term which seems to
embrace not only the senses and the emotions, but also certain
workings of the intellect.

He seems sometimes to think that it is from the examination
of the body, from the nervous system envisaged globally down
to its most simple components, that we may perhaps learn the
real nature of man. In the *cours de poétique*, he puts forward his
views with extreme diffidence, constantly warning his audience
that his suggestions are perhaps misleading, that he has no
means of proving what he says because the subject is so difficult
and his knowledge is not up to the task. He feels helpless and
bewildered before the perspectives which open up to this search
for knowledge about "internité":

> L'homme n'est l'homme qu'à la surface. Lève la peau,
> dissèque: ici commencent les machines. Puis tu te perds dans
> une substance inextricable, étrangère à tout ce que tu sais et
> qui est pourtant l'essentielle. C'est de même pour ton désir,
> pour ton sentiment et ta pensée. La familiarité et l'apparence
> humaine de ces choses s'évanouissent à l'examen. Et si, levant
> le langage, on veut voir sous cette peau, ce qui paraît
> m'égare.[3]

(It is true that, as far as we know, these words were written in
1910, when the nascent science of psychology had disclosed even
less than it has by now. But this defeatism ill becomes a man
who constantly upheld the virtues of will-power and lucidity).
He invites us to think of our

> *vrai milieu*, c'est-à-dire à celui dans lequel et aux dépens
> duquel vivent nos sentiments et nos pensées: il est ce *milieu*
> *intérieur* qui est constitué de notre sang et de nos humeurs, et
> dont la transformation périodique en lui-même, comme ses

---

[1] *Cours de poétique* of 4 March 1938.
[2] *Cours de poétique* of 11 February 1938.
[3] *Cahier B, T.Q. I,* p. 196.

fluctuations de composition, sont les dominantes de notre vie. Dans cet Océan aux orages chimiques, à la salure constante, et de qui la marée a pour astre notre cœur, baignent tous ces éléments nerveux qui sont ce que nous sommes . . . *en tant que nous nous ignorons.*[1]

(The fineness of the metaphor concerning the storms and the tide as well as of the paradox at the end of the quotation is characteristic of many pages of the notebooks. Valéry's talents as a *littérateur* and rhetorician were not so divorced from his private cogitations as he usually liked to think; it might be claimed that these talents were sometimes a hindrance in his search for precision in the fields of psychology and physiology). Human beings are "eux et leurs pensées, sujets de leurs masses cachées," [2] and do not always realize the importance of those "valeurs viscérales . . . irrationnelles . . . le coeur, les glandes, les entrailles,"[3] where there are "quelques gros tyrans qui agissent sans s'expliquer."[4] A study of the nervous system was part of Valéry's programme of universal knowledge; such a study, he once believed, would establish "lois de continuité" [5] with poetry and aesthetics.

Le plus grand poète—c'est le système nerveux. L'inventeur de tout—mais plutôt le seul poète.[6]

According to him, supreme artists must try to understand the working of "internité," with regard both to themselves and their public, to find

les recettes qui leur permettent d'*agir* à coup sûr sur l'être nerveux et psychique,—leur sujet.[7]

But his views on the "fonctionnement d'ensemble" show how

---

[1] *M.P.*, pp. 50, 51.   [2] *Moralités, T.Q. I*, p. 123.   [3] *L'Idée fixe*, p. 79.
[4] *Ibid.*, p. 60. Cf. *Mélange*, pp. 189, 190.
[5] *Introduction à la méthode de Léonard de Vinci, Vinci*, p. 70.
[6] *Mélange*, p. 87.   [7] *Autour de Corot, P.S.L.*, p. 138.

little hope he could reasonably have had of finding many of the
"recettes" in question.[1]

The mind-body relationship and the frontiers between the
two were a constant source of interest and thought for Valéry,
as is well known; this is revealed in his prose no less than in his
poetry. The nervous system provides the tools, so to speak,
without which sensibility or intellect is helpless to act:

> toute la sensibilité du monde, réduite à soi seule, est incapable
> de déplacer un fétu de paille, un grain de poussière. La
> sensibilité se borne à mouvoir quelques éléments du système
> moteur qui obéit comme il peut.[2]

We can thus appreciate that, for Valéry,

> le sensitif et le moteur sont les deux versants de l'être, en
> lesquels presque tout se résout.[3]

In this matter of the nervous system, he seems to have been
especially preoccupied with what, organically speaking, he
considers the simplest and most fundamental elements—certain
"invariants." [4] Jean Hytier has noted what he calls Valéry's
tendency towards "une espèce d'atomisme esthétique," [5]
namely, the notion that a fine poem is composed of isolated
gems of pure poetry; the same tendency is apparent in his
views on "internité," a kind of *atomisme physiologique*, to adapt
Hytier's phrase. Instances of these simple, basic units would be
the nerves and the muscles:

[1] Doubts about the value of his researches assailed Valéry from time to
time. In 1916, for instance, he wrote:
    "Mon travail.
Est-ce que je me trompe?—Me suis-je égaré pendant toute ma vie? Quand
je revois ces cahiers, je vois que j'ai cherché indéfiniment sans but, sans
livre jamais rêvé—ce que je nomme les *conditions de la pensée*." (*Cahiers,
tome sixième*, p. 108).
[2] *Cours de poétique* of 8 January 1938, in *Yggdrasill* of 25 February 1938.
[3] *Ibid.*   [4] *Note et Digression, Vinci*, p. 52.
[5] Jean Hytier, *op. cit.*, p. 112.

Quel personnage extraordinaire que le muscle! C'est le grand mystère de l'organisme. Il ne sait que se raccourcir et se rallonger et toutes nos œuvres sont soumises à ces conditions de muscle.[1]

Simple units is a comparative term: *least complicated* would be better since we know so little, says Valéry, about even a basic element such as the muscle. The important thing for him is that the muscle can perform only two operations: it can contract and it can expand. He concludes that

l'être se divise en parties qui sont de véritables unités, de véritables indivisibles au sens de la sensibilité.[2]

Elsewhere, he expatiates on other "indivisibles," the "pavés sensibles" of the eye. A letter to Pierre Louÿs in 1915 throws interesting light on Valéry's rather mechanistic viewpoint in this matter of functional units:

Figure-toi un cerveau. Ou plutôt un système genre nerveux. (Je n'aime pas le cerveau tout seul: je n'y crois pas). Comme nous ne savons rien sur ce système, il est permis de le regarder comme une myriade de milliards ... de petits industriels distincts. Chacun d'eux ne fait et ne sait faire que ce qu'il fait toujours. Quoi qu'il arrive, il se borne à faire ou à ne pas faire son unique métier. Et il commence ou cesse de le faire sans savoir pourquoi. D'ailleurs il ne sait rien. S'il savait quelque chose, cela reviendrait à supposer qu'il contient lui-même mille milliards d'autres ouvriers. Et ainsi de suite.[3]

He seems therefore to conceive the nervous system as having a kind of hierarchy, rising from the simplest elements (muscle, eye, skin with its sensitive nerves, etc.) through a scale of complexity up to the co-ordinating brain. The brain itself has its hierarchy—it has, so to speak, at the foot of the ladder, reflexes or very simple co-ordinations, while, at the top, there

[1] *Cours de poétique* of 8 January 1938, in *Yggdrasill* of 25 February 1938.
[2] *Cours de poétique* of 11 February 1938. Cf. *Cahiers, tome troisième*, p. 473.
[3] *Quinze lettres de Paul Valéry à Pierre Louÿs*, lettre A.

is the intellect which is capable of very complex and variable co-ordinations.

Valéry stresses above all the relationship of the various elements. No one element functions alone; that is why, as we have noted, the intellect and sensibility cannot be dissociated from each other, functionally speaking.[1] Sensibility is not confined to any one area of "internité" and it is accompanied by all kinds of physiological activity. The essence of "internité" is the interplay of the simplest and most complex elements, and the number of combinations seems unlimited. Valéry, searching for precision and prevision, is taken aback by all these

> possibilités qu'on peut appeler tactiles-motrices, combinaison d'un sens avec un mouvement musculaire, combinées avec sensations tactiles; nous trouvons qu'il existe dans ce groupe une infinité d'associations possibles.[2]

It is not surprising that he often spoke of the need for co-ordination in the various fields of study concerning the "fonctionnement d'ensemble."[3]

The permanence of these preoccupations can be seen clearly if one compares a letter of 1894, to his brother Jules,[4] with the

[1] "Nous ne pouvons dissocier notre existence intellectuelle, même la plus abstraite, d'un soutien de sensibilité profonde" (*Cours de poétique* of 8 January 1938).

[2] *Cours de poétique* of 17 December 1937. Thus, "une idée triste se décompose en une idée qui ne peut pas être triste et une tristesse sans idées" (*Fluctuations sur la liberté, Regards*, p. 83).

[3] Cf. the following words from a lecture given by Valéry at the *Hôpital Bichat*: "Une action humaine est composée de facteurs nombreux qui se coordonnent entre eux pour produire l'action voulue. A ce propos, je me rappelle ce que je disais à un de vos maîtres disparus, le professeur Gley: vous avez fait un traité de physiologie. Ce qui me frappe, c'est que je vois des fonctions différentes qui sont étudiées chapitre par chapitre, mais je ne vois pas une page dans laquelle on fasse allusion à la coordination de tout cela!" (*P.V.V.*, p. 103). Cf. also *Cahiers, tome premier*, p. 105: "La psychologie en tant qu'étude de fonctions, il ne faut pas étudier les portions particulières —discontinues mais les relations générales où le continu peut s'introduire." (written in 1895).

[4] *P.V.V.*, p. 261.

substance of many of the *cours de poétique*. We can believe Valéry when he states:

> la réflexion sur tout sujet me conduit toujours à considérer le point de vue physiologique. Dans tous les ordres des choses, ce qui me paraît le plus important, c'est le fonctionnement.[1]

The striking difference is in the tone, so confident and crisp in the 1894 letter, hesitating and tentative, with frequent reservations, in the *cours de poétique* towards the end of his life. The older he got, the less confident he was of ever fathoming the subject, and the more aware he seemed to become of the difficulties involved; the more he examined, the more he emphasized the limits of the intellect's powers, great though they may be. Thus we can contrast the *Soirée avec Monsieur Teste* (1896) with a sentence from the *Lettre d'un Ami* (1924), in which Valéry states that we are made up of

> bien des choses qui nous ignorent. Et c'est en quoi nous nous ignorons. S'il y en a une infinité, toute méditation est vaine . . .[2]

In 1926, he writes that

> la substance de notre corps n'est pas à notre échelle. Les phénomènes les plus importants pour nous, notre vie, notre sensibilité, notre pensée sont liés intimement à des événements plus petits que les plus petits phénomènes accessibles à nos sens, maniables par nos actes. Nous ne pouvons pas intervenir directement et en voyant ce que nous faisons.[3]

The *cours de poétique* (from 1937 on) carry this awareness of difficulties and the intellect's limitations even further.

In 1938, Valéry confessed that he had cherished the hope of creating a "sorte de dynamique sensorielle, esthésique," [4] that

---

[1] *Paul Valéry et la médecine*, by P. Chardon, p. 22.
[2] *Lettre d'un ami, Teste*, p. 93.   [3] *Analecta, T.Q. II*, p. 250.
[4] *Cours de poétique* of 26 March 1938.

is, an aesthetic based on the study of sensation. Under the heading of "esthésique," he would put

> les travaux qui ont pour objet les excitations et les réactions sensibles *qui n'ont pas de rôle physiologique uniforme et bien défini*.[1]

He admitted that he had never realized this dream, not in its entirety, at least, and in 1938, at the age of sixty-seven, he no doubt felt it was rather late to be thinking of doing so. But "c'est une limite vers laquelle on essaierait de tendre."[2] We have Valéry in epitome here—the initial ambition or dream associated with his "mystique intellectuelle," the gradual realization that the goal is really unattainable, the persistence none the less of the ambition and, as we shall see later, the accumulation of details derived from the study involved in the ambition, what one might call in his own phrase, da Vinci-like "débris d'on ne sait quels grands jeux."[3]

He says explicitly that he refers to

> une dynamique fondée sur l'observation et non pas sur les observations de laboratoire.[4]

In ordinary, physical mechanics, he tells us, one works on a prepared, chosen, isolated field from which have been excluded as far as possible any influence or phenomena alien to the experiment in progress. The physicist can construct the apparatus he wants to work on, and this facilitates his work enormously.[5] Valéry's own position is very different. He is not the first to discover that observation of "internité" can never be detached, or sections of it isolated for controlled experiment. He claims that he has had to combine in himself the functions of specialists who work in various fields—semantics, etymology, psychology, psychiatry, letters—specialists who work separately at present.[6] His programme has been this:

---

[1] *L'Esthétique, Var. IV*, p. 264.
[2] *Cours de poétique* of 26 March 1938.
[3] *Introduction à la méthode de Léonard de Vinci, Vinci*, p. 64.
[4] *Cours de poétique* of 11 March 1938. [5] *Ibid.* [6] *Ibid.*

J'ai essayé de me faire une idée plus simple et aussi utilisable que possible de l'être vivant. Non pas du mécanisme intime, profondément caché, qui se découvre ou se soupçonne à l'échelle de la cellule, du noyau, etc. Non plus le mécanisme plus intime encore qui consiste dans les modifications et les échanges d'ordre moléculaire. Je suis trop ignorant pour même y songer et je pense que ce ne serait pas pour moi d'une utilité immédiate. Ce que je voudrais me représenter, c'est le mécanisme à notre échelle, et en particulier les actions réciproques du système nerveux, du système musculaire, des glandes et de leurs sécrétions, dans leurs rapports immédiats avec les variations qui se produisent dans le système nerveux. C'est le *mot-à-mot* de la vie, la génération des instants successifs, en quelque sorte, le domaine dans lequel nos passions, nos émotions, toutes les transformations de notre vie perçue, se passent.[1]

Valéry's avowed ignorance is, of course, quite understandable. But how, being so ignorant, can he possibly hope to achieve his declared ambition? He does not claim to be scientific. He cannot obtain and, perforce, does not want facts which, for him, are unintelligible and unusable, truth which applies only to a narrow field of experience. He wants to know more about the "fonctionnement d'ensemble" not as a specialist, but as an "homme universel" (however dim the original vision of such a creature may have become). A general view, expressible in terms as simple, recognizable and everyday as possible, could be related to his life, his other knowledge, his experience of art and poetry.

He believes that

la réalité à l'état nu est insignifiante, c'est-à-dire sans aucune signification.[2]

It is we who, through our "fonctionnement d'ensemble," impose our patterns on external reality. According to this

---

[1] *Paul Valéry et la médecine*, by P. Chardon, pp. 23, 24.
[2] *Cours de poétique* in *Yggdrasill* of 25 December 1938.

commonplace of idealistic philosophy embraced by Valéry, reality has no meaning unless there is an observer; it is an inexhaustible field of objects and phenomena; [1] it is everything minus man, or rather, minus one man, since no man sees exactly like another. Valéry thinks that if our perceptions were fine enough, infinitely acute, there would be no such thing as repetition for us. This conception of reality is inherent in his solipsistic philosophy. It is the foundation of his views concerning the way body and mind function.

*

The general theories we have examined form a background for a number of particular theories which are of special interest for our study of inspiration and technique.

We have seen that Valéry notes the existence of certain basic elements, "indivisibles," such as the muscle. Functionally speaking, in the realm of sensibility within the nervous system, the important "indivisible" is what he calls on different occasions the "moi de l'instant," [2] the "moi fonctionnel"[3] or the "moi instantané." [4] This self is

une négation en acte . . . il repousse à chaque instant ce qui vient d'être lui, et surtout ce qui vient d'être lui.[5]

It is opposed both to the stimuli from outside the body and to the sensibility inside.[6] He was aware that this self was a schema imposed by himself and he compared it to the

centre de gravité d'un corps creux, sphère ou anneau, notion

---

[1] Cf. *Cahiers, tome huitième*, p. 408: "Le 'réel' est ce qui est capable d'une infinité de 'points de vue'."

[2] *Cours de poétique* of 12 March 1938.

[3] *Cours de poétique* of 11 February 1938, in *Yggdrasill* of 25 August 1938.

[4] *Cours de poétique* of 11 February 1938.

[5] *Cours de poétique* of 12 March 1938.

[6] *Cours de poétique* of 11 February 1938, in *Yggdrasill* of 25 August 1938. Valéry says: "A chaque instant, notre moi lui-même est une sorte de réponse à l'hétérogénéité, à la diversité de la sensibilité générale."

abstraite, centre qui joue un rôle essentiel et cependant n'existe pas. Notre moi fonctionnel est de même nature, à la fois abstrait et existant. Ce point vivant et abstrait, ce moi étant et n'étant pas, on peut le considérer lui-même comme une fonction, la fonction supérieure de la sensibilité.[1]

The "moi instantané" exists only from second to second, during certain short periods which are "indivisibles;" as with the organic "indivisibles," when we examine them, we find they consist of a stimulus and a response, and are rarely both these things at the same time.[2] The "moi instantané" has no memory and cannot perform any operation. It is purely functional.[3] Valéry calls it the "recul du coup de canon qu'est la sensation." [4] After a very short space of time, it grows richer and more complex until it becomes one with our whole personality.[5] He says that the interval of time separating the "moi instantané" from the internal process of enrichment must be a few hundredths or tenths of a second.[6] In a manner which recalls to a degree that of an I. A. Richards or a J. E. Downey, Valéry states that the sensation is received

dans un champ de possibilités très différentes: ... il faut imaginer une sorte d'espace dans lequel se propage cette première impulsion, qui nous est donnée par la sensation. Et alors cet espace est très loin d'être homogène, il rencontre des résistances différentes en certains points: il y a des points, des voies plutôt, des directions dans lesquelles il peut s'égarer et se perdre, s'amortir, et d'autres dans lesquelles il peut

[1] *Cours de poétique* of 11 February 1938, in *Yggdrasill* of 25 August 1938.
[2] *Cours de poétique* of 11 February 1938.
[3] *Cours de poétique* of 12 February 1938.
[4] *Cours de poétique* of 18 February 1938. In *Cahiers, tome troisième*, p. 149, we read: "Au fond la sensation est un *choc*—une annihilation très courte de la conscience—la perception venant après.
"La sensation doit détruire qq. chose–Elle contient un élément énergétique de la nature d'un choc."
[5] *Cours de poétique* of 18 February 1938.
[6] *Cours de poétique* of 5 March 1938.

produire des retentissements qui, eux-mêmes, seront l'origine de nouvelles perturbations.[1]

It is thus clear that, for Valéry, as for Condillac and the *sensualistes*, all knowledge in the last analysis is based on the material furnished by sensation.

He thinks there are various autonomous and, as it were, closed structures of sensations. He speaks of a "universe of colours," [2] and supposes that there are different "worlds" of sensibility, that there are as many worlds as there are types of closed sensations. Thus

> il y a deux mondes, un monde visuel, un monde auditif, comme il y a un monde de sensations tactiles ... nous pouvons considérer qu'ils sont entièrement cloisonnés.[3]

These worlds are susceptible of two very different activities. In the "ordre des choses pratiques"

> il semble que la grande affaire de notre vie soit de remettre au *zéro* je ne sais quel index de notre sensibilité, et de nous rendre par le plus court chemin un certain *maximum* de liberté ou de disponibilité de notre sens.[4]

If we have the sensation of hunger, we eat, and the sensation of hunger disappears as the need to eat is satisfied: the gamut of

[1] *Cours de poétique* of 11 March 1938.

[2] *L'Infini esthétique*, P.S.L. 1948, p. 203. His observation of the complementary nature of the gradation of colours striking the retina was probably the point of departure for his notion of the "aesthetic infinite." See *L'Infini esthétique* just mentioned. In *Autour de Corot*, P.S.L., p. 151, Valéry affirms that "certains phénomènes... nous font concevoir la sensation comme premier terme de développements harmoniques," while in *Cahiers, tome huitième*, p. 690, he writes: "Chose poétique = celle qui fait que ns lui répondons par une improvisation de sentiments, d'attentes, d'images constituant un monde intense ou plus profond, qui tend à se régénérer sans cesse, se recommencer—comme les complémentaires de l'œil... C'est une création propre et oscillante."

[3] *Cours de poétique* of 18 December 1937.

[4] *L'Infini esthétique*, P.S.L. 1948, p. 201.

sensations set in being by the need is annulled by the satisfaction of the need and sensibility returns to the state of "availability" already mentioned. But, in aesthetic experience, the worlds of closed sensations tend to maintain an unceasing activity. Certain of our impressions impose themselves to such an extent that we seek to renew them.[1] In the domain of art, man seems to have created "une utilité de second ordre," [2] where satisfaction begets more desire. "Infini esthétique" is the term Valéry humorously coined to characterize the universe of sensibility in which a sensation and the seeking after it exert a kind of reciprocal action, the one pursuing the other indefinitely.[3]

Another factor stressed by him is the importance of motor sensations. They obviously enable the process of enrichment beyond the stage of the "moi instantané" to take place.[4] Most of our activities involved motor sensations, often when there is no actual action or discernable movement of the body. Valéry seems to be thinking not merely of the suppressed vocalization which occurs when reading poetry, but also of the potential imagined movement in our "internité," the theory of which is discussed, for instance, by I. A. Richards in his *Principles of Literary Criticism*.[5] The consideration is particularly important for the effect of rhythm in poetry.

[1] *Cours de poétique* of 17 December 1937.
[2] *Ibid.* Cf. *Cahiers, tome sixième*, p. 208: "L'art transforme les moyens et les change en fins. Ainsi le langage, les sensations."
[3] *L'Infini esthétique, P.S.L.* 1948, p. 203.
[4] *Cours de poétique* of 11 March 1938.
[5] Thus we read in *Cahiers, tome deuxième*, p. 138: "Nos muscles *suivent* en quelque sorte le mouvement de la pierre jetée que l'œil regarde voler, et *imaginent*, ou le jet de la pierre, ou l'effort qu'elle semble faire de soi-même pour changer de lieu. Cela est comprendre." When it is a question of artistic appreciation, Valéry seems to have had in mind the activity described by June E. Downey in her book *Creative Imagination* (Studies in the Psychology of Literature), London, Kegan Paul, Trench, Trubner & Co. Ltd., 1929, p. 46: "The lines of a statue or building release certain movements of accommodation, certain kinaesthetic and organic patterns of perception which as integral parts of an emotional complex reinstate this complex in the act of contemplation."

It seems, then, that within "internité," the stages of development are from sensation to impression, from impression to perception, from perception to thought, from thought to group of thoughts, from group of thoughts to habits or habitual states, from habitual states to personality or character: the intellect—and, particularly, its highest manifestation, 'awareness',—can transcend all these developments. Each stage marks an increase in complexity and the progression from what Valéry called "le sensitif" to "le psychique": each stage involves physiological activity and affective elements. It is important to note that, at the perception stage, there is no difference between the artist or poet and the scientist. The difference comes later, when the perception has been received into the "field of possibilities"[1] constituted by the nervous system in general. In a man who has spent his life studying science (a man who had initially, one assumes, innate gifts for such work), the perception will naturally tend to produce thoughts or an internal reaction which will be expressed in scientific terms. And likewise for the poet. This fact has some significance in Valéry's theories concerning the amount of conscious self-preparation possible to the artist.

It is difficult, if not impossible, Valéry affirms, to control or understand the stages which follow an initial impression:

> Rien de plus incertain, rien de plus difficile à prévoir que ce qu'il adviendra de la trace laissée en nous par un événement de la sensibilité ... Rien n'explique l'inégalité du destin de nos impressions, et il semble qu'une sorte du hasard se joue de ce que nous fûmes comme il fait de ce que nous serons.[2]

He compares our mind and nervous system to a solid body on a plane that never finds a position of stable equilibrium.[3] He does not know what factors decide how a sensation will be received into the nervous system, nor how and with what intensity a sensation becomes associated with motor elements. He does

---

[1] *Cours de poétique* of 11 March 1938. [2] *Mélange,* pp. 103, 104.
[3] *Cours de poétique* of 8 January 1938.

make one positive point, namely, that sensibility gives birth to
an enormous number of *moi*. The simplest is the "moi instantané:" our thoughts, groups of thoughts (attitudes), habits
and character can be envisaged as so many groupings, so many
conglomerations of selves based on the "moi instantané." The
time factor is very important:

> Je conviens qu'il y a plus d'une personne en nous. Il y en
> a une, par exemple, qui n'apparaît que dans des intervalles
> d'un dixième de seconde, ou d'un vingtième. Et une autre
> qui ne peut produire ses effets que moyennant un temps un
> peu plus long.[1]

These selves can come together to form groups which compose
our habitual states, our character, no doubt by dint of what
might be called frequency tracks (J. E. Downey calls them
"mental sets")[2] formed in the field of connections and possibilities which Valéry envisages the nervous system to be. In this
manner, several of these composite selves can have latent
existence in one person. Hence Swedenborg, in Valéry's
opinion, contained at least two "moi composés:"

> Comment ne pas voir que nos formations spirituelles font
> partie du groupe des combinaisons qui peuvent se composer
> en nous à partir de nos acquisitions sensorielles et de nos
> possibilités et libertés psychiques et affectives? Tandis que
> Svedenborg *savant* avait certainement considéré le monde
> sensible comme l'aspect superficiel d'un monde physico-
> mécanique selon Descartes ou selon Newton, Svedenborg
> *mystique* considérait cet aspect sensible superficiel, d'intuition
> naïve, comme expression d'un monde 'spitiruel'.[3]

As we saw from Valéry's conception of reality, each of us can
have only our habitual, or more or less habitual, glimpses of
an inexhaustible reality. Everyone must conceptualize and abstract, and hence have a greater or lesser number of "mental

---

[1] *L'Idée fixe*, pp. 81, 82.
[2] J. E. Downey, *op. cit.*, p. 167.
[3] *Svedenborg, Var. V*, p. 276.

sets."¹ On this question, his viewpoint might be considered as not far removed from that of *Gestalt* psychology, according to which we necessarily perceive phenomena in organized wholes, patterns, precisely because reality is too complex to be faced otherwise if we are to think and live.² At the lowest level, most people are too dominated by habit, unavoidably perhaps, to the extent that they have to earn a living and hence

> la vision utile ne retient que ce qui peut avoir une significa-tion, une valeur d'action.³

Valéry clearly implies that 'awareness' can, by being con-scious of this determinism, attempt to transcend it, if only to a limited extent. So he affirms:

> Toutes choses sont étranges. Et l'on peut toujours les ressen-tir dans leur étrangeté, dès qu'elles ne jouent aucun rôle; que *l'on veut ne rien trouver qui leur ressemble,* et que leur *matière demeure.*⁴

These words (published in 1930) sum up much of his method, in the later years especially, though they hark back to the da Vinci myth. His da Vinci could at will return from glorious abstractions

---

¹ Cf. *M.P.*, p. 211: "nous ne pouvons penser, combiner, calculer, con-jecturer qu'en négligeant la plus grande partie de ce que nous percevons, et la totalité de ce que nous ne percevons pas."

² Cf. *Cahiers, tome cinquième,* p. 232: "Tout point de vue néglige, sup-prime une partie de ce qui est. Mais l'absence ou la pluralité de points de vue est ou interdite ou conduisant à l'impotence mentale par confusion et impossibilité d'agir." Cf. also *Cahiers, tome troisième,* p. 330: "Le besoin psychologique est de fabriquer son objet—faire des objets sur quoi on puisse opérer au lieu de ce domaine falot." Thus, if we put various men in a stretch of countryside, "un philosophe vaguement n'apercevra que *phéno-mènes;* un géologue, des époques cristallisées, mêlées, ruinées, pulvérisées; et ce ne serait pour un paysan que des hectares, des sueurs et des profits" (*Tante Berthe, P.S.L.,* pp. 174, 175).

³ *Cours de poétique* of 17 December 1937, in *Yggdrasill* of 25 January 1938.

⁴ *Moralités, T.Q. I,* pp. 93, 94.

aux ivresses de l'instinct particulier et à l'émotion que donne la moindre chose réelle.[1]

The ideal poet must be able to do this: he must be able to theorize but also to experience the force and strangeness of concrete reality. When Valéry states that three quarters of the mind's time is spent in ridding itself of habitual responses,[2] we must understand that this precept was capable of the widest possible application. He tells us, for instance, that we can consciously try to interpose a delaying process at the stage of the simple sensation, the "moi instantané," to prevent too habitual associations of ideas and feelings. One cannot be confident of the results of such an operation, but by this means, we may find that there is

> un accrochage, une résistance, et alors qu'à partir de cette résistance rencontrée, il y ait développement dans des sens qui n'étaient pas attendus.[3] [Car] c'est avant que nous ayons achevé la connaissance qui va nous conduire jusqu'à la mémoire ... aux clichés, qui vont nous débarrasser de l'impression, avant que nous arrivions à cette chose toute faite et toute digérée par notre esprit, que nous avons chance de trouver quelques notions, quelques voies nouvelles sur cette sorte de chemin des possibilités successives.[4]

Habits, habitual states, "mental sets"—it is scarcely possible to distinguish between these groupings, which are not exactly fixed, but may change slowly or quickly according to circumstances. But a distinction can be drawn between these and states or groupings of states which are merely potential, requiring favourable circumstances to become actual: for the potential groupings Valéry uses the expression "l'implexe:"

---

[1] *Introduction à la méthode de Léonard de Vinci, Vinci*, p. 76. Cf. also *Note et Digression, Vinci*, p. 27: Da Vinci "n'a pas peur des analyses; il les mène—ou bien ce sont elles qui le conduisent—aux conséquences éloignées; il retourne au réel sans effort."

[2] *Mélange*, p. 191.

[3] *Cours de poétique* of 12 March 1938.   [4] *Ibid.*

L'Implexe n'est pas *activité*. Tout le contraire. Il est *capacité*. Notre capacité de sentir, de réagir, de faire, de comprendre.[1]

In one of his *cours de poétique*, he explains that "implexe" covers two things: the functions themselves, i.e. the simple physiological and organic reactions, and also the co-ordinations of these functions, our "groupements."[2]

The question of habit is closely linked with what he calls our "états d'attente,"[3] which can vary greatly in their power, depending on how many of the elements of the "fonctionnement d'ensemble" are involved; at their most powerful, they invariably entail the activity of motor nerves. To illustrate his idea, he instances the man sitting in a crowded hall who has had a foreboding that fire might break out; this foreboding will have changed his internal "availability," so that, if a fire did actually break out, he would act more quickly and effectively than others. As is often the case in these matters, Valéry does not or cannot go into the physiological detail; he can only note the fact that there is "un montage intérieur dont nous ignorons les conditions."[4] The "états d'attente" have their importance in his ideas both about the stages of poetic creation and about the condition of "internité" in the reader of poems.

We saw that, according to Valéry, when "internité" is affected by stimuli, it tends to return as quickly as possible to its former state of "availability." He speaks of

une tentative de reprise, de retour à la disponibilité générale de nos ressources et de nos énergies,[5]

and uses the term "cours naturel" to describe this normal state of general "availability." The "cours naturel" is

une sorte de régime plus ou moins permanent et régulier[6]

---

[1] *L'Idée fixe*, p. 104.   [2] *Cours de poétique* of 19 March 1938.
[3] *Cours de poétique* of 18 February 1938. Valéry explains that "à chaque instant, nous sommes accommodés, sans nous en douter, à des phénomènes qui peuvent se produire et non à d'autres".
[4] *P.V.V.*, p. 104.   [5] *Cours de poétique* of 11 March 1938.
[6] *Cours de poétique* of 18 March 1938.

... un état qu'on pourrait appeler d'indifférence fonction-
nelle, un état dans lequel des substitutions, des impressions
sont assez conformes au régime fonctionnel le plus normal,
le plus économique, pour ne pas éveiller les ripostes pro-
fondes, les changements d'états ... car la conséquence d'une
atteinte plus forte sur nos sens, c'est d'amener un changement d'état.[1]

It is that comfortable, habitual state of incoherence into which
"internité" slips back after some effort or action.[2] No sensation,
no group of sensations is in the ascendancy during the "cours
naturel." This state Valéry opposes to what he calls "le monde
de l'attention" or "la phase," that particular organization
of "internité" which is formed when there is some act to
accomplish, when one of the internal groupings assumes the
ascendancy and everything else is subordinated to it.

"Energie nerveuse" or "énergie psychique"[3] is a term used
by Valéry to describe the force which serves as a kind of
catalyst in most of our internal activities.[4] He believes that
everyone has a certain quantum of energy to expend, depending on one's physiological and nervous constitution:

L'absurde et son contraire participent des mêmes forces. La
nature nous verse un quantum qu'il lui est indifférent que
nous dépensions, (ou qui se dépensât) en sottises ou en
miracles d'intelligence.[5]

He says elsewhere that

[1] *Cours de poétique* of 4 March 1938.
[2] It is "l'état de... non-attention, qui est évidemment le plus fréquent...
c'est un état dans lequel tout peut se substituer à tout. La suite de la vie
psychique, si on l'enregistrait, montrerait un désordre, une incohérence...
parfaite" (*L'Idée fixe*, p. 37).
[3] *Cours de poétique* of 4 February 1938.
[4] Cf. *Cahiers, tome deuxième*, p. 203: "Système—Les phénomènes
mentaux n'ont pas une énergie propre mais ils utilisent une énergie générale
—spéciale."
[5] M.P., p. 21.

nous pouvons enfanter autant de difficultés que nous avons
envie de dépenser d'énergie psychique . . . le définitif d'une
solution dépendrait généralement, en toute matière où il n'y
a pas de vérification extérieure, de notre poussée de sensibilité, de la quantité, si vous voulez, d'énergie psychique qui
veut s'employer, qui est à ce moment-là à notre disposition.[1]

Hence one finds Valéry seeing himself as 'working off' so
much energy, as when, in a letter of 1940, he explains that he is
working at his *Faust*, which will never be finished, simply to
use up time and energy, like a horse pawing the ground.[2]
He has

> jours à idées [qui] seraient . . . des jours où une *richesse* encore
> indéterminée, non attribuée—abonderait dans l'état de l'être
> pensant—comme l'*énergie utilisable*, libre, surabonde dans le
> cheval qui piaffe et s'impatiente.[3]

He believes that an expenditure of this energy is usually an
integral part of any feeling of well-being, happiness:

> A quel 'Signe' un artiste connaît-il qu'il est, à tel instant,
> dans son 'Vrai'? et perçoit-il la nécessité en même temps
> que la volupté (et toutes deux croissantes) de son acte créa-
> teur?—Le *Signe* de SVEDENBORG n'était peut-être que la
> sensation d'énergie, de plénitude heureuse, de bien-être qu'il
> éprouvait toujours à se laisser produire et organiser son
> monde spirituel . . .[4]

If poetry is to attract the reader and give him a sense of well-
being, it must involve a certain high expenditure of this energy.

[1] *Cours de poétique* of 4 February 1938.   [2] *P.V.V.*, p. 97.
[3] *Mélange*, p. 55. His account of rhythmical inspiration in *Poésie et pensée
abstraite*, *Var. V*, pp. 140, 141, contains the following remark: "J'ai imaginé
que la production mentale pendant la marche devait répondre à une
excitation générale qui se dépensait du côté de mon cerveau; cette excitation
se satisfaisait, se soulageait comme elle pouvait, et, pourvu qu'elle dissipât
de l'énergie, il lui importait peu que ce fussent des idées, ou des souvenirs,
ou des rythmes fredonnés distraitement."
[4] *Svedenborg*, *Var. V*, p. 280.

Valéry believes this is best achieved when the poetry makes an appeal to the whole of man's "internité:"

> La poésie doit s'étendre à tout l'être; elle excite son organisa-tion musculaire par les rythmes, délivre ou déchaîne ses facultés verbales dont elle exalte le jeu total, elle l'ordonne en profondeur.[1]

He stresses the participation of the whole person, including the physiological part.

The complexity and the interdependence of all the various elements of "internité" are so great that it would be impossible to accomplish the simplest act if full consciousness of all that its accomplishment entailed were necessary.[2] The body, all those elements at the lower end of the scale, muscles, etc., if they are to work at all well, must work to a large extent 'in the dark' and not be uncovered by the intellect:

> le système nerveux est Autruche. Il rougit, il se cache sous le sang, *qui le fait voir*. C'est une sorte de bêtise, de naïveté physiologique.[3]

> Toute émotion tend à voiler le mécanisme toujours niais et naïf de sa genèse et de son développement.[4]

Valéry concludes that

> l'esprit ne doit donc pas se mêler de tout,—quoiqu'il se soit découvert cette vocation. On dirait qu'il n'est fait que pour ne s'employer qu'à nos affaires extérieures. Quant au reste, à nos activités de base, une sorte de raison d'état les couvre . .. Soyons distraits pour vivre.[5]

Such platitudes, redeemed to some extent by the occasional brilliant aphorism, show Valéry grappling with the notion that some processes are necessarily unconscious. When he concedes that

---

[1] *Propos sur la poésie, Conf.*, p. 80.   [2] *Cours de poétique, Var. V*, p. 301.
[3] *Analecta, T.Q. II*, p. 214.   [4] *Mélange*, p. 104.
[5] *Discours aux chirurgiens, Var. V*, p. 53.

peut-être le vague est indestructible, son existence nécessaire
au fonctionnement psychique,[1]

the obstinate "peut-être" is characteristic. These admissions
confirm his later acceptance of the fact that the poet cannot
know and control vital elements in himself and in his reader.
But the mature Valéry, despite this concession which is quite
foreign to his earlier "mystique intellectuelle," thinks that the
poet can be less dependent on "le vague" than his reader. It is
all a matter of degree. His earlier dream of dominating the
reader still remains. The indispensability for all humanity of
varying degrees of "le vague" is linked with his belief in the
weakness of most people's intellect and the existence in their
minds of "myths," or "seuils infranchissables à la pensée;"[2]
their minds can think so far and then boggle and give up. For
most people,

tout repose sur quelques idées qui se font craindre et qu'on
ne peut regarder en face.[3]

These few ideas are their beliefs. For Valéry, a belief is a myth,
since

une croyance est une abstention des puissances · de notre
esprit, lequel répugne à se former toutes les hypothèses
concevables sur les choses absentes et à leur donner à toutes
la même force de vérité.[4]

He does not favour belief; he prefers "l'éternellement pro-

---

[1] *Analecta, T.Q. II*, p. 298.   [2] *Suite, T.Q. II*, p. 326.
[3] *Choses tues, T.Q. I*, p. 68. Cf. *Introduction à la méthode de Léonard de
Vinci, Vinci*, p. 84: "Penser consiste, presque tout le temps que nous y
donnons, à errer parmi des motifs dont nous savons, avant tout, que nous
les connaissons *plus ou moins bien*. Les choses pourraient donc se classer
d'après la facilité qu'elles offrent à notre compréhension, d'après le degré
de familiarité que nous avons avec elles, et selon les résistances diverses que
nous opposent leurs conditions ou leurs parties pour être imaginées ensemble.
Reste à conjecturer l'histoire de cette graduation de la complexité."
[4] *Mon Faust*, p. 25.

visoire." [1] Everyone has myths (even Valéry, though he clearly thinks he has less than most). They are related to the force of habit and the lack of 'awareness':

> Ni morale ni de moralistes sans une certaine organisation réflexe qui termine et domine l'intellect. Il faut que la pudeur, la honte, l'indignation, l'euphorie des idéaux, la sensation du juste et de l'injuste, soient des seuils infranchissables à la pensée.[2]

The important fact is that these beliefs, these myths, necessary for life and action, usually involve much of the person's "internité." We do not find a belief alone, existing as a purely rational entity, but a belief sustained and maintained by all the nervous energy and complexity of the "fonctionnement d'ensemble." [3] Our individual quantum of energy can be used in actions of an external nature or activities predominantly internal, particularly thinking, but in the latter case, the myths or "seuils infranchissables à la pensée" prevent the energy from spreading to the highest part of the intellect, 'awareness'. The rôle of language is vital in this respect. For Valéry, a given word or phrase may correspond to a certain myth in a man's mind. A word like *amour* or *Dieu*, accompanied by a few affective adjectives, is enough to rouse into activity a whole affective world,[4] involving much of the "internité," functioning on a basis of psychic energy—because 'awareness' is scarcely in-

---

[1] *L.Q.*, p. 245.   [2] *Suite, T.Q. II*, p. 326.

[3] Such a combination Valéry termed an "accommodation"—an adjustment of various elements of "internité". Complex "accommodations" were one of his constant studies (See, for a typical mention of this theme, *Cahiers, tome troisième*, p. 519). Speaking of ideas in *Cahiers, tome huitième*, p. 182, he refers to "leur propriété d'être clefs de notre énergie." In *Analecta, T.Q. II*, p. 281, he affirms that "croire à une chose, c'est pouvoir ou devoir ajouter à l'idée de cette chose, une capacité de résister et de faire agir, extérieure à cette chose même. Une énergie d'emprunt."

[4] Such words are, like "Volonté, Idée, Clarté, Nécessité, Liberté, Universalité... des *mots-clefs*, ...des *mots-seuils*" (*Cahiers, tome huitième*, p. 527). The logical analysis of the Viennese Circle and of philophers such as Wittgenstein and Ayer has by now made Valéry's idea fairly commonplace.

volved. The magic of literature, he says, is largely founded on these myths.[1] Such "thresholds" are found in every field of human knowledge and experience.

Toute politique voit avant tout des fusillades massives; puis le bonheur universel,[2]

because the upper, conscious regions of "internité" have not been able to fathom the business of politics. There are as many myths as there are patterns of reality, which in turn depend on men's different sensibilities and nervous systems. Thus Valéry talks of

la sensibilité politique, la sensibilité religieuse, la sensibilité confessionnelle, la sensibilité scientifique,[3]

which all vary according to the individual's inborn nature and his training, education and experience. These myths betray —by Valéry's standards—the confusion occurring in man, because of the existence in him of contradictions in ideas, feelings, impulsions, which he resolves (if he tries to resolve them at all) from minute to minute, from day to day, as best he can; often, he cannot resolve them because he does not have the necessary time or intellect to do so. So long as a make-shift compromise is reached, so long as nervous energy is expended, people 'get by', the more so because they are usually not

[1] Cf. Fragments des mémoires d'un poème, Var. V, p. 95.
[2] Choses tues, T.Q. I, p. 72. In Cahiers, tome quatrième, p. 294, we read: "L'éducation, l'âge, l'abêtissement, des aventures—agissant sur l'appareil le plus sensible du moi—finissent par rendre tabous certains chemins de la pensée et interdire certaines précisions. Des signaux étranges sont installés qui dès l'approche de certaines idées, comme mus par leur simple mise en mouvement, encore soient-elles cachées, font développer le trouble et obscurcissent l'eau du diamant mental—pour refuser l'état d'intellect à telles images, impossibiliser tels calculs comme dangereux et 'défiant Dieu', redissoudre telles prévisions et résorber tels souvenirs—en tant que à leur sujet, le vague vaut mieux que le net, l'oubli que l'être.
"...Mais éclairées à fond, ces choses (comme les autres) seraient des enfers de carton. Et sans la sensibilité tout combinaisons, tout équivalents."
[3] Cours de poétique of 11 March 1938.

conscious of all these factors, of these actual contradictions in their natures.

*

The most ardent admirer of Valéry could not shut his eyes to the pompous platitudes which mar some of his assertions about the "fonctionnement d'ensemble." In our account, we have drawn considerably from certain of the *cours de poétique*. Though they are a transcript of what he actually said at the *Collège de France*, Valéry did not intend them to be published in this state.[1] It appears that he did not read them word for word; he improvised to some extent. These factors may account for a certain laxity of style. The nebulous and arbitrarily personal terms or schemes of thought he sometimes used can be seen as an attempt to rationalize his acceptance of the limitations of 'awareness' and technique, the existence of "le vague" and, by implication, inspiration. "Le vague" and "la sensibilité" comprehend, among other things, feeling, the nature, functions and importance of which he does not adequately analyse. The element of pseudo-scientific verbiage undoubtedly present in the lectures is partly explained by the fact that Valéry, distinguished poet and aesthetician though he may be, was clearly not always at ease in this field where psychology, physiology and philosophy overlap, and that he was trying to explain things which are not easy to explain at all, and especially difficult to explain in a limited time to a composite audience. Moreover, we have been able to refer to only a small number of the lectures: the others have not to our knowledge been preserved.

Nevertheless, Valéry's views on the "fonctionnement d'ensemble" will be useful in our subsequent chapters because, as we have noted, they will help us to understand the essential background of his thought concerning both the composition and the enjoyment of poetry. He clearly meant his lectures to provide this background. The poet's deliberate attempt to

[1] Madame Valéry told us this.

cultivate his talent and augment his versatility, the stages of creation and the skilful subjugation of the reader will be the more easily and fully appreciated. The acceptance of technique's limitations makes his detailed analyses of poet and reader all the more valuable, given the *volonté de tout comprendre* which he never really abandoned.

CHAPTER III

POETRY AND THE READER

T HE mature Valéry's views on the question of inspiration and technique are to be found in scattered writings; they seem to amalgamate theories and attitudes from the 1890s and the so-called period of silence with other theories and attitudes which resulted from his full return to poetic creation in 1913. Our main interest will naturally be in his views on the poet's functioning, but it is essential first to examine his ideas concerning poetry and the reader, in so far as they constitute a part of his ideas about technique. The more consciously such theories about poetry and the psychology of the reader can be applied by the poet, the less room there is for inspiration. Valéry, it must be remembered, had his own personal view of what poetry was and what kind of poetry he wished to write; his theories are naturally coloured by this personal taste. He was quite aware that there is more than one kind of poetry and more than one kind of poet.[1] It will therefore be useful to begin by recapitulating very briefly the attitude he took towards poetic creation in writings published after 1917.

The residue of the early "mystique intellectuelle" is apparent in the attitude towards poetic creation revealed by the older Valéry. He shows at times a certain contempt for literature because

> l'homo scriptor, l'homme de la plume ne peut qu'il ne songe à l'effet sur un lecteur de ce qu'il impose au papier. Il spécule inconsciemment ou non sur le pouvoir des mots.[2]

Writing is irreconcilable with the search for truth and universal knowledge, whether about life and art or about oneself. "Comment plaire et se plaire?"[3] The writer cannot avoid

---

[1] Cf. *Fontaines de Mémoire*, *P.S.L.* 1948, pp. 246, 247.

[2] Valéry's preface to *Les Chimères* of Nerval, Paris, Les Amis de la poésie, 1944, p. 17.

[3] *Fragments des mémoires d'un poème*, *Var. V*, p. 80.

being something of an actor and his medium is inevitably a mixture of intellect and sensibility obnoxious to that part of Valéry which still hankers after his youthful ideal. "En littérature, le vrai n'est pas concevable." [1] The pervasiveness of the earlier "mystique intellectuelle" and the consequent attitude to literature are perhaps even more clearly revealed in a statement of 1927, when he explains that the mere idea of composing a literary work occasions

> je ne sais quel ennui de se dépenser à spéculer sur l'inexact et à tenter de provoquer autrui à des émotions et à des pensées étonnantes et tout imprévues pour nous-mêmes, comme le seraient les conséquences d'un acte irréfléchi. Ces réactions incalculables du lecteur fussent-elles (comme il arrive) favorables à notre ouvrage, et quand elles seraient infiniment douces à notre vanité heureusement surprise, l'orgueil profond se plaint d'être offensé dans sa rigueur.[2]

Valéry said some hard things about poetry, which seemed scandalous to many. In 1922, he wrote to André Gide:

> Je m'en fous, moi, de la poésie. Elle ne m'intéresse que par raccroc. C'est par accident que j'ai écrit des vers.[3]

In 1936, he wrote:

> le métier d'écrire m'inspirait même un étrange éloignement, qui dure encore.[4]

Why then did he write and publish so much from 1917 onwards? Are these statements mere humbug?—The young Valéry had a faith in science and, at the same time, in the powers of intellect and analysis, much stronger than that of the mature Valéry. Poetry was considered by the young man as mytho-

---

[1] *Stendhal, Var. II*, p. 127.   [2] *Lettre sur Mallarmé, Mall.*, p. 41.

[3] Extract from André Gide's journal, in *Paul Valéry*, by Gide, Paris, Domat, 1947, p. LXXV.

[4] Preface to *Papiers*, by Edouard Julia, Paris, Editions du Temps, 1936, p. 2. Cf. also *L.Q.*, p. 207: "mon intention n'a jamais été d'être ce que je suis devenu par le fait des autres."

pœic in a way science or intellectual analysis was not. In later years, he seems to think all is, to a large extent, myth, including the findings of science and intellectual analysis. It has already been noted that he grows to feel there is a deep gulf set between *la partie* and *le tout*, the individual man and reality. Poetry thus, to put it crudely, comes back into its own. In the words of I. A. Richards (writing in quite another context):

> While any part of the world-picture is regarded as not of mythopœic origin, poetry—earlier recognized as mythopœic—could not but be given a second place. If philosophic contemplation, or religious experience, or science gave us Reality, then poetry gave us something of less consequence, at best some sort of shadow. If we grant that all is myth, poetry, as the myth-making which most brings 'the whole soul of man into activity' . . . becomes the necessary channel for the reconstitution of order.[1]

For Valéry, poetic composition confers two benefits: the first is concerned with the understanding and the second with moral values. During composition, he acquires knowledge about himself and art, especially knowledge in the form of principles which enshrine operations both verifiable and repeatable at will.

> J'ai jugé, à un âge fort tendre, et j'ai pris comme programme personnel, l'augmentation de conscience des opérations de l'esprit, appliquant ceci à la poésie.[2]

[1] I. A. Richards, *Coleridge on Imagination*, London, Routledge and Kegan Paul, 1934, p. 228.

[2] *La Création artistique*, *Vues*, p. 309. Cf. also L.Q., pp. 123, 124: "le véritable bénéfice tiré par moi de cette *Parque*, réside dans des observations sur moi-même prises pendant le travail." Since the 1890s, Valéry's attitude to poetic composition has changed indeed. In 1937, he can write: "On voit que la préoccupation de l'effet extérieur était subordonné à mes yeux à celle du 'travail interne'" (*Fragments des mémoires d'un poème*, *Var. V*, p. 105. The past tense refers to the time of composition of *La Jeune Parque*, 1913–1917). In 1894, it was precisely the "effet extérieur" which constituted the biggest single preoccupation of the Valéry inspired by his reading of Poe. The *volte-face* is, however, more apparent than real. We need to speak rather of

His moral criteria are personal: clarity, detachment, self-reliance. Thus for him a fine book is

> celui qui [lui] donne du langage une idée plus noble et plus profonde ... Cette manière de sentir conduit à juger de la littérature en général, et de chaque livre en particulier, selon ce qu'ils supposent ou suggèrent de présence et de liberté d'esprit, de conscience, de coordination et de possession de *l'univers des mots*.[1]

It is not the completed work and its fortune in the world which benefit the poet, but only the process of its composition.[2] He was fond of envisaging composition as an "exercise"[3] or a "game"[4] because by composition he is changed

> en quelqu'un de plus indépendant à l'égard des mots, c'est-à-dire, plus maître de sa pensée.[5]

Many poets since the beginning of the nineteenth century have sought as their main goal what has been termed self-knowledge or self-expression. They compose poetry because it is for them the only medium in which they can objectify the complex and intimate depths of their nature. Valéry is one of them:

> Ce n'est pas le *nouveau* ni le *génie* qui me séduisent,—mais la possession de soi.—Et elle revient à se douer du plus grand

---

a modification of attitude as he transfers his attention from the end—poetic production, the poem—to the means. We have seen already how this change came about and the reasons for it.

[1] *Littérature, T.Q. I*, pp. 180, 181.

[2] *Lettre sur Mallarmé, Mall.*, p. 38. Cf. also *Fragments des mémoires d'un poème, Var. V*, p. 102: "Je m'intéresse beaucoup plus à savoir produire à mon gré une infime étincelle qu'à attendre de projeter çà et là les éclats d'une foudre incertaine."

[3] *Propos*, p. 49.   [4] *Ibid.*

[5] *Ibid.* Cf. Lefèvre, *Entretiens avec Paul Valéry*, p. 54: "La littérature ne satisfaisait pas mon esprit de ce moment-là. Je m'habituais à la considérer comme une activité partielle dont l'objet supérieur est l'étude et l'acquisition des moyens d'expression par le langage."

nombre de moyens d'expression, pour atteindre et saisir ce Soi et n'en pas laisser perdre les puissances natives, faute d'organes pour les servir.[1]

He appears, here as elsewhere, to have systematically carried further a tendency present in poets before him. Part of his originality is that he has two selves: the one which was responsible for the theorizing consigned to his notebooks and the other for the nascent ideas, often tinged with strong emotion and a certain compulsion, destined to end in a poem. He seeks to apply the same attentive method to both selves, which are not kept so separate as he imagines. When dealing generally with his poetic composition, he often tends, consciously or unconsciously, to speak of his method and not enough of the nature of his second self.

He claimed that all he wrote after 1892 was written to order or by request.[2] In point of fact, Le Cimetière Marin and La Jeune Parque do not appear to have been composed in response to any request (unless he means, with reference to the second of the two poems, that his original notion of a farewell to poetry—the origin of the poem, he says—was asked for in that Gide and Gallimard wanted to form a collection of his early poems, which occasioned the notion of a farewell and hence the poem). Certainly no one asked him to take such pains for so long over La Jeune Parque. By his own confession, several of his poems started with 'intermittent inspiration' (such as Le Cimetière Marin and La Pythie). In his later years, such is the persistence of youthful attitudes and dreams in their attenuated form, Valéry wants to think, and wants perhaps others to think, that his poetic composition is even more methodical and willed than it really is. An interesting example is his account of the genesis of Le Cimetière Marin. The vagueness of this account is apparent. The words "démon de la généralisation," "une certaine strophe," "une diversité de tons et de fonctions," suggest rather than explain a methodical composition in the

[1] Rhumbs, T.Q. II, p. 95.
[2] Lefèvre, Entretiens avec Paul Valéry, p. 54.

manner of Edgar Allan Poe. There is question-begging in the lines:

> Entre les strophes, des contrastes ou des correspondances devaient être institués. Cette dernière condition exigea bientôt que le poème possible fût un monologue de 'moi', dans lequel les thèmes les plus simples et les plus constants de ma vie affective et intellectuelle ... fussent appelés, tramés, opposés ...[1]

As L. J. Austin points out in his study of the poem, there is no necessary connection between decasyllabic stanzas of six lines and the poem's themes.[2]

Valéry's firm distinction between poet, poem and reader[3] is too well known to need treatment here. The ensuing ambiguity of the word *poésie* does, however, have great importance for our present considerations. He notes that the word can signify

> un certain genre d'émotion, un état émotif particulier, qui peut être provoqué par les objets ou des circonstances très diverses.[4]

Poetry in this sense thus refers to the "poetic state" or "poetic emotion" which we have labelled as 'intermittent inspiration'. This state comes and goes quite capriciously:

> tout le monde connaît cet ébranlement spécial comparable à l'état dans lequel nous sommes lorsque nous nous sentons, par l'effet de certaines circonstances, excités, enchantés. Cet état est entièrement indépendant de toute œuvre déterminée et il résulte naturellement et spontanément d'un certain

---

[1] *Au sujet du Cimetière Marin, Var. III*, p. 64.

[2] *Paul Valéry: Le Cimétière Marin. Introduction d'Henri Mondor, Genèse du Poème par L. J. Austin*, Grenoble, Roissard, 1954—pages not numbered.

[3] *La Création artistique, Vues*, pp. 293, 294.

[4] *Propos sur la poésie, Conf.*, p. 64. Cf. also *Poésie*, p. IX: "Poésie, terme équivoque, veut dire parfois: Affection qui tend à créer; et quelquefois; Production qui tend à nous affecter."

accord entre notre disposition interne, physique et psychique, et les circonstances (réelles ou idéales) qui nous impressionnent.[1]

He is anxious to distinguish between this special emotion and emotions generally. He is thus led to define 'intermittent inspiration' more clearly:

Il nous importe d'opposer aussi nettement que possible l'émotion poétique à l'émotion ordinaire. La séparation est assez délicate à opérer, car elle n'est jamais réalisée dans les faits. On trouve toujours mêlées à l'émoi poétique essentiel la tendresse ou la tristesse, la fureur ou la crainte ou l'espérance; et les intérêts et les affections particuliers de l'individu ne laissent point de se combiner à cette *sensation d'univers* qui est caractéristique de la poésie.

J'ai dit: *sensation d'univers*. J'ai voulu dire que l'état ou émotion poétique me semble consister dans une perception naissante, dans une tendance à percevoir un *monde*, un système complet de rapports, dans lequel les êtres, les choses, les événements et les actes, s'ils ressemblent, *chacun à chacun*, à ceux qui peuplent et composent le monde sensible, le monde immédiat duquel ils sont empruntés, sont, d'autre part, dans une relation indéfinissable, mais merveilleusement juste, avec les modes et les lois de notre sensibilité générale. Alors, ces objets et ces êtres connus changent en quelque sorte de valeur. Ils s'appellent les uns les autres, ils s'associent tout autrement que dans les conditions ordinaires. Ils se trouvent,—permettez-moi cette expression,—*musicalisés*, devenus commensurables, résonnants l'un par l'autre.[2]

The poetic state ushers in

un *monde fermé* où toutes choses *réelles* peuvent être représentées, mais où toutes choses paraissent et se modifient par les seules variations de notre sensibilité profonde.

[1] *Calepin d'un poète, Poésies*, pp. 202, 203.
[2] *Propos sur la poésie, Conf.*, p. 65.

The state, Valéry thinks, can be experienced by many people who do not necessarily write poems (or compose music, or paint), who do not necessarily produce as a result even "fragments" of verse, words or rhythms to be clothed in words.

These definitions reveal very clearly that Valéry theorizes about poetry as an aesthetician, and equates the true poetic experience with a peculiarly intellectual and aesthetic one. Art and life are separate for him; he said on various occasions that he disliked 'life' in art, and spoke of eliminating or transcending "le désordre monotone de la vie extérieure." [1] It is not surprising, therefore, that he should see 'intermittent inspiration' as an essentially aesthetic experience, but one which has an inevitable admixture of impure, ordinary emotion (the latter tends to link the inspired person with 'ordinary' life and other people). The real core of 'intermittent inspiration' ("l'émoi poétique essential") is an aesthetic experience, both self-contained and self-sufficient, even though the elements of the experience are in fact derived from 'ordinary' life. The experience is self-generating and self-controlling (a "monde fermé"), in that it is the "variations de notre sensibilité profonde" which govern its existence. It is to be explained, or at least, described, in terms of aesthetics, physiology and psychology. In other words, we have here an account of Valéry's "aesthetic infinite," though this phrase is not mentioned. (One assumes the phrase had not yet been coined by Valéry. The *Propos sur la poésie*, from which the above quotations are taken, first appeared in 1928, the article on *L'Infini esthétique* in 1934).

The second sense of the word *poetry* is much narrower than the first and signifies that activity during which one attempts to

> restituer l'émotion poétique à volonté, en dehors des conditions naturelles où elle se produit spontanément et au moyen des artifices du langage . . . [2]

Valéry's distinction between the two senses of the word is summed up admirably in his phrase:

[1] *Fragments des mémoires d'un poème, Var. V*, p. 108.
[2] *Propos sur la poésie, Conf.*, p. 64.

Sentir n'emporte pas *rendre sensible,*—et encore moins: *bellement sensible.*[1]

He no longer attempts to claim that poetry can be composed without any form of initial impetus or emotion—the so-called "poetic state" or "poetic emotion" is essential to the composer —but he does stress that the poet needs both "une sorte d'émotion" and a certain talent, an evaluative talent which comprehends an intimate acquaintance with, and control of, language. He affirms quite simply that if poetry is

> dans son principe une sorte d'émotion, elle est un genre singulier d'émotion qui veut se créer des figures.[2]

For Valéry, poetry is a certain way in which man's sensibility is stimulated and kept going. It is perhaps best defined by its very difference from prose. The aim of prose is a finite mental modification of the person to whom the prose is addressed: its aim, in other words, is comprehension, and as soon as that is achieved, the medium whereby it has been achieved is ignored or forgotten. The efficacy of the prose is judged by the ease with which the message the prose transmits becomes a part of the knowledge of the person addressed and independent of the particular form of the prose used.[3] The aim of poetry, he says, is very different. Poetry aims at creating a mood, a certain state; it does not aim at the accomplishment of some action, nor does it aim at a finite modification of the internal state of the reader. Poetry begins at the point where we pay attention to and are affected by the form which the language takes:

> aussitôt que cette forme sensible prend par son propre effet une importance telle qu'elle s'impose, et se fasse, en quelque sorte, respecter; et non seulement remarquer et respecter, mais désirer, et donc reprendre—alors quelque chose de nouveau se déclare: nous sommes insensiblement transformés, et disposés à vivre, à respirer, à penser selon un régime

---

[1] *Questions de poésie, Var. III,* p. 38.   [2] *Poésie,* pp. XI, XII.
[3] *Poésie et pensée abstraite, Var. V,* pp. 143, 144.

et sous des lois qui ne sont plus de l'ordre pratique—c'est-
à-dire que rien de ce qui se passera dans cet état ne sera
résolu, achevé, aboli par un acte bien déterminé. Nous
entrons dans l'univers poétique.[1]

There are thus two extremes—pure prose and pure poetry.
Pure poetry is at the opposite pole from prose, suppressing
utterly all data derived from discursive or empirical knowledge.[2] Pure poetry, ideally, would have no 'subject' at all, but
since this is impossible, then the subject would be as near to
being absent, would be as insignificant, as "fragile"[3] as possible. In fact, however, pure poetry remains an ideal for Valéry;
poetry is never or rarely so pure that some thought or idea or
fact does not inevitably enter, and for the good. It is clear that
normally, for him, the sense or content of a poem is as important as its form or the state which it must induce in the reader.
Poetry, he claims, has two functions:

> Transmettre un fait—produire une émotion. La poésie est
> un *compromis*, ou une certaine proportion de ces deux
> fonctions.[4]

Sound and sense, form and content, production of emotion and
transmission of fact must be indissolubly wedded, a condition
indicated in one of his best descriptions of poetry—"cette
hésitation prolongée entre le son et le sens."[5] Given Valéry's
eminently sound view of the indissolubility of sound and

---

[1] *Ibid.*, p. 144.   [2] *Situation de Baudelaire, Var. II*, p. 166.
[3] *Littérature, T.Q. I*, p. 145.
[4] *Je disais quelquefois à Stéphane Mallarmé, Mall.*, p. 51.
[5] *Rhumbs, T.Q. II*, p. 79. Cf. also Valéry's preface to the *Poèmes* of
Ladislas Mécs, Paris, Horizons de France, 1944, p. XIV: "moins un
ouvrage est poétique, moins est-il altéré par sa traduction. La poésie est une
tentative toujours téméraire de rendre indissolubles la forme et le fond d'un
discours." In an excellent description of this indissolubility, Valéry affirms
in *Cahiers, tome troisième*, p. 412 that "le *son* du vers donne la température
pour laquelle le *sens* est le plus suggéré, imprimé et *mû* dans l'auditeur. Le
son déchaîne l'état énergétique grâce auquel le sens se réalise—et devient,
de notation et de traduction, chose vécue."

sense in good poetry, (and of form and content), it can be claimed that the sense is so transformed by its new associations and the new synthesis achieved that it is qualitatively different from the sense of discursive prose. The sense is "musicalized," to use Valéry's expression, and thereby is achieved that constant oscillation between, on the one hand,

> la forme, les caractères sensibles du langage, le son, le rythme, les accents, le timbre, le mouvement—en un mot, la *Voix* en action

and, on the other hand,

> toutes les valeurs significatives, les images, les idées; les excitations du sentiment et de la mémoire, les impulsions virtuelles et les formations de compréhension—en un mot, tout ce qui constitue le *fond*, le sens d'un discours.[1]

His ideal was far removed from that of poets who seek to communicate as directly as possible ideas or feelings they have themselves experienced. He sought a continuation and extension of Mallarmé's aim: "peindre non la chose, mais l'effet qu'elle produit" [2]—the careful building-up in words of intense states of soul, mind, sensation, the creation of "enchantement" and "charmes" at concentrated pressure, a highly charged poetic "machine" worthy of Poe's theorizings. The pleasure to be derived from such an intense poetry was to be as nearly

---

[1] *Poésie et pensée abstraite, Var. V*, p. 152.

[2] Mallarmé, letter of October 1864 to Cazalis, in Mondor, *Vie de Mallarmé*, Paris, Gallimard, 1946, pp. 145, 146. In 1910, Valéry wrote: "Le vrai 'symbolisme' entièrement différent de l'allégorie consiste à déterminer une chose ou un état, en provoquant le même réflexe qu'elle provoque. Plus généralement, on place le patient dans des conditions telles qu'il ne peut manquer de produire l'image ou l'état que l'on veut qu'il éprouve.

"Il résulte de cette définition que le nom de la chose même doit plutôt être *évité*, car c'est tarir en sa source l'excitation que l'on cherche à produire, que de la nommer" (*Cahiers, tome quatrième*, p. 489). The debt to Mallarmé is evident. Cf. also *Cahiers, tome huitième*, p. 642: "Les arts d'*imitation* ont pour objet non de *reproduire* les choses (comme leur nom le ferait croire) mais de *produire* l'*effet* ou tel effet que les choses produisent."

"pure" [1] as possible, a "ravissement sans référence," [2] akin to that obtained by Valéry from Mallarmé's poetry, in that such poetry was to be a very sophisticated and self-conscious exploitation of all the powers of language. The best readers, the 'happy few', would share with the poet the awareness of the self-conscious exploitation of these powers as well as the richness of those states of exaltation which is indissociable from language itself so exploited. (From occasional remarks made by Valéry, it would appear that, according to him, many readers, perhaps all save an élite, benefit from the richness of the states of exaltation but cannot fully share with the poet the actual awareness of the deliberate linguistic exploitation he has achieved). Valéry clarified what we have referred to briefly as 'states of exaltation' when he wrote that poetry

> réalise l'exaltation simultanée de notre sensibilité, de notre intellect, de notre mémoire et de notre pouvoir d'action verbale, si rarement accordée dans le train ordinaire de notre vie. [3]

He expressed his ideal succinctly in the following passage:

> La littérature n'est rien de désirable si elle n'est un exercice supérieur de l'animal intellectuel.

[1] Cf. Valéry's advice to writers in *Cahiers, tome troisième*, p. 116: "Au lieu de vouloir faire *croire* faites simplement et directement imaginer, raisonner... donnez [au lecteur] votre pensée comme pensée—et laissez le trompe-l'œil à la populace.—Se décrire soi-même a commencé cette réforme. Mais depuis toujours, le vers, l'étrange métrique, par son conventionnel système—montre avec franchise presque brutalement,—le but, qui est d'*enchanter* sans tromper." Deception is equated with reference to facts, with mere description and with the intrusion of "le désordre monotone de la vie extérieure."

[2] *Fragments des mémoires d'un poème, Var. V*, p. 107.

[3] *Poésie et pensée abstraite, Var. V*, p. 160. He argued that poetry should make us feel "la possession de la plénitude des pouvoirs antagonistes qui sont en nous" (*Fragments des mémoires d'un poème, Var. V*, p. 106), that poetry brings about "l'heureux succès de la participation à une œuvre de toutes les facultés de l'homme" (*Le Physique du livre*, Valéry's preface to the book *Paul Bonet*, Paris, Auguste Blaizot, 1945, p. 24).

Il faut donc qu'elle comporte l'emploi de *toutes* les fonctions mentales de cet animal; prises dans leur plus grande netteté, finesse et force et qu'elle en réalise l'activité combinée, sans autres illusions que celles qu'elle-même produit ou provoque en se jouant.[1]

Another phrase by Mallarmé seems to describe most aptly the kind of poetry Valéry admired and strove to create:

elle [la poésie] est éprise d'elle-même, et . . . sa volupté d'elle retombe délicieusement en mon âme.[2]

Valéry defined post-romanticism as the substitution of a spontaneous act by a deliberate one.[3] In various writings,[4] he showed how conscious he was of belonging to a certain poetic development, beginning essentially with Baudelaire, which he characterized as

la recherche de la poésie même [dont la] profondeur est possession de plus en plus intime, de plus en plus précise, de tous les moyens d'un art dont l'objet, ou si vous voulez, la fin, est dans une relation très étroite avec ses moyens.[5]

Valéry consciously developed to their extreme consequences principles which were only in germ in other poets,[6] particularly those with regard to the "charme" or "enchantement" already preconized to some extent by Poe, Baudelaire and Mallarmé, the brevity and density of poetic effect, the attention to form until it ousts, or rather, overlaps content, and, at the same time, the (inevitable) necessity of painstakingly critical evaluation at all stages of composition at the expense of so-called inspiration.

---

[1] *Rhumbs, T.Q. II*, p. 72.
[2] Mallarmé, letter of May 1867 to Cazalis, in Mondor, *Vie de Mallarmé*, p. 238.
[3] *Situation de Baudelaire, Var. II*, p. 150.
[4] Cf. *Existence du symbolisme, Mall.*, pp. 123–126: *Remerciement à l'Académie Française, Discours*, p. 16: *Avant-Propos pour la Connaissance de la Déesse, Var.* 1948, p. 112.
[5] Lefèvre, *Entretiens avec Paul Valéry*, p. 68.   [6] Cf. L. J. Austin, *op. cit.*

In fine, given his preoccupations and his poetic ideal, 'total inspiration' was necessarily dismissed; 'intermittent inspiration' and 'intuitive inspiration' were essential and were to be used to some extent, though always circumspectly and subject to a general evaluative process,—they were, in other words, to be exploited with care and effort; 'exalted inspiration' was well known to Valéry and we shall see in the next chapter that this kind of inspiration is envisaged as the fruit of much thought and training, however difficult it may be for the observer to distinguish between it and the forms we have called 'total', 'intermittent' and 'intuitive'. He thinks that 'attributed inspiration', associated with value-judgement, operates with the majority of readers, but much less with those who are well acquainted with the problem of poetic creation as seen by him.

*

Since the "aesthetic infinite" constitutes for Valéry the essence of the poetic state experienced by the reader, the problem for the poet becomes: how to evoke sensations and keep them in a perpetual state of activity? Valéry believes that the "esprit" (or the "intellect," for he uses the two words indifferently in this connection) has a great influence over all our "internité," and, therefore, over all the sensations; it is the head of the hierarchy which we examined in our second chapter. Consequently, the intellect must be appealed to, must be kept in a state of activity such that it cannot bring this state to an end. If it does so, then it tends by its very power and influence to terminate also the activity of the rest of "internité," and hence of all the other sensations set in motion by the poem. This amounts to stating that the reader must not believe that he has completely understood the poem, or rather, must not believe that he has 'exhausted' it, that he can define the impressions which it has created:

> Toute chose dont on peut se faire une idée nette perd de sa force de prestige et de sa résonance dans l'esprit.[1]

[1] *Fonction et mystère de l'Académie, Regards II*, p. 292.

Une chose ne vaut que dans la mesure où elle échappe à l'expression. Il faut que tout ce que l'on peut en dire n'en puisse épuiser la notion.[1]

When prose is heard or read, the nervous system is stirred into activity and the reader or listener enters the "phase" or "monde de l'attention" in view of the action which is to be carried out, or the idea which is to be understood; once the action is accomplished or the words understood, the particular organisation of the "internité" ceases, and the reader or listener returns to the state which Valéry calls the "cours naturel." [2] It follows that

tout ce que nous pouvons définir se distingue aussitôt de l'esprit producteur et s'y oppose. L'esprit en fait du même coup l'équivalent d'une matière sur quoi il peut opérer ou d'un instrument par quoi il peut opérer. Ce qu'il a bien défini, l'esprit le place donc hors de ses atteintes.[3]

The intellect, by its very nature, always seeks to put an end to indecision and any state of "sensibilité entretenue." If the intellect succeeds in getting back to the "cours naturel," sensibility must do the same and there is no room for the "aesthetic infinite." The problem, therefore is to suppress, or rather, to keep under control this tendency of intellect, and the problem is set forth clearly in a page of *Analecta*:

Un ouvrage donne une impression. Si elle est définissable et classable, elle est *finie*. On s'en défera par un acte classificateur. Mais s'il faut *pour sa durée*, et pour atteindre une certaine intensité et un certain effet esthétique, qu'il hante la mémoire, qu'il ne soit pas résumable, ni facile à définir, qu'il n'y ait pas d'acte qui le satisfasse,—trouver les conditions de cet ouvrage et les assembler dans le réel, c'est ce qu'on appelle la magie, la beauté.[4]

And Valéry adds at the foot of the page:

En somme, les dimensions d'un ouvrage doivent être déter-

---

[1] *Ibid.*, p. 299.   [2] *Cours de poétique* of 18 March 1938.
[3] *Cours de poétique*, *Var. V*, p. 309.   [4] *Analecta*, T.Q. *II*, pp. 282, 283.

minées par une analyse des conditions de prolongement, de renforcement et de répétition des impressions.

The poet foils the classifying act of the intellect, and hence ensures the continuity of the "aesthetic infinite," by various means, above all by appealing sufficiently to the intellect to 'set it going' and by never letting it fonction predominantly alone; in other words, by appealing strongly to all that is not intellect in the reader—emotions, rhythmical sense, as many as possible of those elements of the "fonctionnement d'ensemble" which were mentioned in our second chapter. If this appeal is powerful enough, the intellect has difficulty in returning to the "cours naturel;" if it does struggle to do so, it struggles in vain against the "heureux succès de la participation à une œuvre de toutes les facultés de l'homme" [1] which the composite appeal of the poem has achieved. In his own poetry, Valéry intensifies elements obviously inherent in all poetic language. Thus he often chooses themes or 'problems' which, by their nature, and along with the particular form in which they are expressed, excite the intellect, but which, as themes, do not lend themselves to clear-cut notions, or, as 'problems', are incapable of definitive solution—the conflict between being and knowing in *La Jeune Parque* or *Le Cimetière Marin* would be a good instance.[2] Such themes can be developed into "une cime, un point suprême de l'être," [3] one of those "seuils infranchissables à la pensée" [4] which introduces the reader into a world of interaction between sensibility and the intellect. They lend themselves most readily to that "hésitation prolongée entre le son et le sens" which characterizes Valéry's poetic ideal. If the fusion between sound and sense, between values of intellect and values of sensibility, is achieved by the poet, then

[1] See p. 75, note 3.
[2] There are various formulations of this conflict in Valéry's prose. Here is a typical one, from *Cahiers, tome quatrième*, p. 683: "L'homme ne résisterait pas à une connaissance extrême de soi. Car ce qui veut être et ce qui veut connaître se détruisent mutuellement."
[3] *Propos sur la poésie, Conf.*, p. 76.
[4] *Suite, T.Q. II*, p. 326.

Valéry's "poetic pendulum" [1] operates; the intellect cannot isolate the prose or sense element in the poem and the "aesthetic infinite" is not destroyed. He thus believes that a certain amount of difficulty is necessary in a poem. (Valéry claimed, and truthfully, that what difficulty his readers found in his poems was what he had been unable to avoid, given his conception of poetry. He did not say to himself—"I must introduce some difficulty here or there." The difficulty, for the intellect alone of the reader, was inherent in his conception of poetry —as an appeal to the whole man—which governed his composition from the very start of a poem). The difficulty must not be too great, or the reader will be completely discouraged and give up. The themes must be recognizable to the reader, he must be able to think about and around them, he must be attracted to them; the appeal to all the elements of "internité" other than intellect must be strong enough for him not to be able to use the intellect's classifying act as on a piece of prose.

If we bear in mind certain points which emerged in the last chapter, it is clear that the "fonctionnement d'ensemble" reveals certain powerful aids for the poet in his attempt to foil the intellect.

In the first place, although the intellect influences and, to a considerable extent, co-ordinates our whole "internité," there is no doubt that it does not altogether control it; certain elements escape. [2] This fact applies particularly to the physiological side of our being—one immediately thinks of certain reflexes which, by definition, are beyond control. Some parts of our being have to work 'in the dark' to work at all. Valéry thinks this is especially true of the emotions. In fact,

> nous sommes enclins à donner une importance *absolue* aux choses qui provoquent en nous des effets physiques tout *irrationnels*—Entre tous les objets, celui que distingue un pincement au cœur qu'il nous cause,—une chaleur aux

[1] *Poésie et pensée abstraite*, *Var. V*, p. 152.
[2] Cf. *Cahiers, tome cinquième*, p. 458: "La conscience règne et ne gouverne pas."

joues,—une sécheresse de la gorge,—un suspens de notre souffle,—celui-là *compte ;* il masque les autres; et les anéantit sur le moment.[1]

These functions are of the greatest importance in the arts since they can be called into play to foil the intellect's classifying rôle.

But there is a still greater aid for the poet in his attempt to control the latter—the limited power of the intellect in most people, those "seuils infranchissables à la pensée:"

C'est un grand avantage pour un poète que l'incapacité où la plupart des êtres se sentent de pousser leur pensée *au delà* du point où elle éblouit, excite, transporte. L'étincelle illumine un lieu qui semble infini au petit temps donné pour le voir. L'expression éblouit. La merveille du choc ne peut se distinguer des objets qu'il révèle. Les ombres fortes qui paraissent dans l'instant demeurent au souvenir comme des meubles admirables. On ne les discerne pas des vrais objets. On en fait des choses positives. Mais observe bien que, par un grand bonheur pour la poésie, le *petit temps* dont j'ai parlé ne peut se dilater; on ne peut substituer à l'étincelle une *lumière fixe entretenue. Celle-ci éclairerait tout autre chose.* Les phénomènes ici dépendent de la source éclairante. Le *petit temps* donne des lueurs d'un autre système ou 'monde' *que ne peut éclairer une clarté durable.* Ce monde . . . est essentielle-ment *instable.* Peut-être est-ce le monde de la *connexion propre et libre* des ressources virtuelles de l'esprit? Le monde des attractions, des plus courts chemins, des résonances . . .[2]

The time factor is very important. According to Valéry, it is a vital fact that we cannot think of one thing for long, nor can we think of two things at one and the same time.[3] These

---

[1] *Moralités, T.Q. I,* p. 120.   [2] *Mélange,* pp. 192, 193.

[3] *Cours de poétique* of 22 January 1938. Cf. *Cahiers, tome deuxième,* p. 41: "La plus grande source d'erreur en psychologie est de confondre ce dont l'esprit est capable pendant une certaine quantité de temps avec ce dont il

facts can be linked with the "phénomène photo-poétique," [1] to use his term, which has just been described, to give us a clearer idea of what happens in the "internité." Impressions derive from the "moi instantané," from sensations which are fresh, often startlingly powerful, and end up with the comprehensive self,[2] the grouping which embraces the intellect, where they are weighed, clarified and annulled. If the "aesthetic infinite" is to exist and endure, there must be some stop along the path which leads from the "moi instantané" to the comprehensive self. He points out that the nature of metaphors illustrates this need of a halt along the path. How are metaphors formed? He says that

> elles se produisent précisément par voie d'arrêt sur la route des possibilités—choses inachevées et incomplètes.[3]

If the impression—which gives the metaphor—did the whole journey from the "moi instantané" to the comprehensive self, it would cease to exist, for the intellect would assemble the necessary precise facts to show that the resemblance originally believed to exist is only an illusion. The halt can be brought about, in poetry, as we have seen, by the appeal made to all that is not intellect in the reader, but the fact that many or most people's intellect cannot get beyond certain thresholds can also help to cause this stop.

The thresholds can be linked with ideas, feelings, images, beliefs, to become myths which are so desirable or so important to us that we never question them. If some object or association conjuring up one of these myths appears (a word, particularly), the myth influences in a very real sense the whole "internité." There is stimulus and an activity which cannot die away through the agency of the classifying intellect, precisely because the threshold exists. The activity, and the psychic energy

---

est capable dans un temps plus long ou plus court." The same idea is expressed in almost identical language in *Cahiers, tome premier*, p. 389.
[1] *Mélange*, pp. 192, 193.   [2] Valéry calls it "le moi complet."
[3] *Cours de poétique* of 12 March 1938.

accompanying it, tend therefore to spread to the whole "inter-nité," particularly to those parts at the bottom of the nervous system's hierarchy according to Valéry—the blood, nerves, muscles, etc.[1] Once the impression has been received,

> la pensée inarticulée, avortée, refusée [par le seuil] irrite ce qu'elle peut, se dégrade en effets locaux presque au hasard.[2]

Rhythm is another aspect of the time factor which bears on the "aesthetic infinite." Rhythms make a direct appeal to our organic functions. Valéry always stressed the importance of motor sensations. There seems to be a very close relationship between them and rhythms, the latter communicating intense activity to the former. Rhythms, in other words, help to foil the intellect's classifying function. During the reading of a poem, all the activity in the reader's "internité" takes place at a certain speed imposed by the rhythm of the verse.

> Le poème oblige notre voix, même intérieure, à se dégager du ton et de l'allure du discours ordinaire, et la place dans un tout autre mode et comme dans un tout autre *temps*.[3]

As with music, the rhythm of the poem is associated with the profound resonances set in motion in the reader. The latter is prevented from exhausting the poem's potential because of the complexity with which the poem has been put together, and because the rhythm and a certain imposed speed keep him 'on the move'. He neither wishes nor finds it possible to submit the ideas and impressions received to the examination of the classifying intellect working alone and unhindered. Thus Valéry affirms that, in poetry, the ideas we find are

> celles qui ne sont possible que dans un mouvement trop vite,

---

[1] This seems to be the diffusion, but in reverse, of an activity described by Valéry when he affirmed that "il y a des parties organiques, composées de parties moindres et telles que si une de ces parties moindres est en activité les autres le sont aussi—Ainsi une fibre dans un muscle—une région de la rétine et la rétine" (*Cahiers, tome troisième*, p. 235).

[2] *M.P.*, p. 203.   [3] *Cantiques spirituels, Var. V*, p. 172.

ou rythmique, ou irréfléchi de la pensée . . . la poésie a pour objet spécial—l'expression de ce qui est inexprimable en fonctions finies de mots.[1]

The nature of language also helps the poet to control the intellect. Valéry imagines—doubtless with every justification— that most readers are not so critical of language as he is, are not so conscious of its mythical nature. The reader's reaction to the written word might be described thus:

> Au commencement est la confusion, même quand on ne l'aperçoit pas. Il arrive trop souvent que la recherche se développe à partir de cet état, volant aux solutions avant d'avoir *nettoyé* ce *champ mental*.[2]

What Valéry deplores as a reaction to prose, when the concern is with information or truth, is a help in poetry. This confusion is so much ground lost by the classifying intellect. The element of emotivity in language for most people prevents the intellect from fixing and defining. In view of Valéry's theories about myths and his general view of the "fonctionnement d'ensemble," it is evident that

> la compréhension d'un mot 'courant' est . . . fonction de celui qui doit le comprendre, de son bagage intellectuel, de sa richesse associative, de son état affectif présent ou re-mémoré, bref de variables qualitatives ou quantitatives, plus ou moins associées, suivant le jeu imprévisible de la formule individuelle du 'récepteur', du 'consommateur'.[3]

Our individual reactions to language help to foil the intellect. Though the phrase "jeu imprévisible" in the quotation implies that it is difficult to predict the effect language will have, certain words seem bound to be proof against the intellect:

---

[1] *Calepin d'un poète, Poésies*, pp. 186, 187. Cf. *Analecta, T.Q. II*, p. 212: "Ce qu'il y a d'excitant dans les idées n'est pas idées; c'est ce qui n'est point pensé, ce qui est naissant et non né, qui excite."

[2] *La Création artistique, Vues*, pp. 292, 293.   [3] *P.V.V.*, p. 225.

Le mot 'pain', en soi, mot chose, mot utilitaire, mot d'usage, a moins de possibilités que le mot 'liberté', par exemple, car il s'ajoute un minimum de conditions extérieures dans son adaptation au langage courant, tandis que 'liberté' implique toute une gamme d'états affectifs possibles.[1]

Valéry seems to think that certain abstract words are often the best suited to create the "aesthetic infinite." According to him, the word *spirituel* in Swedenborg is a good illustration of the effect an abstract word can have:

Spirituel est un mot-clef, un mot dont la signification est une résonance. Il ne dirige pas l'esprit vers un objet de pensée mais il ébranle tout un milieu affectif et imaginatif réservé.[2]

In the same way, the word *pur* is potentially poetic,

si beau qu'il emporte l'âme au delà de toute signification finie. Il excite, par une sorte de résonance, un éblouissement intellectuel, un éveil mystérieux de toutes les puissances supérieures de l'être.[3]

Of course, abstract words are not *ipso facto* suitable for inclusion in a poem. To merit this, they must conform to Valéry's general *desiderata* of poetry. He avoids abstract words which are too technical or specialized.[4] (This is particularly the case with *La Jeune Parque*). Multiplicity of meaning and of effet [5]

---

[1] *Ibid.*, p. 224.

[2] *Svedenborg, Var. V*, p. 274.

[3] *Discours à l'inauguration d'une plaque commémorative du séjour de M. Henri Brémond, 18 Rue Chanoinesse*, p. 7.

[4] Cf. *Cahiers, tome sixième*, p. 469: "A mon sentiment, il est essentiel d'exclure de la poésie (*en général*), tous les mots avec lesquels on ne pense pas. Les *mots* qui *seraient ridicules à chanter*. Les mots non familiers à la pensée, comme irradier, etc. Les mots qui ne viennent pas sans sembler être cherchés. Il faut du travail pour leur faire la chasse et simuler les premiers termes de la *pensée à l'état naissant*. Simulation aussi savante que l'on peut, de la pensée à l'état naissant. C'est poésie."

[5] Cf. *Cahiers, tome troisième*, p. 864: "Symbolisme poétique. Le symbolisme (le nôtre) est simplement l'usage, l'utilisation habile de la pluralité de

—the ambiguity which has been such a preoccupation of certain English critics in recent years—is what Valéry constantly sought, whether the language is abstract or concrete. Thus the abstract significance of many of his poetic themes is conveyed by concrete and sensuous imagery.

If we bear in mind all the considerations examined in our second chapter, it is clear enough that

l'état du lecteur de poèmes n'est pas l'état du lecteur de pures pensées.[1]

The reader of poetry enters "le monde de l'attention," "la phase." His sensibility is not in that state of "availability" which Valéry calls "le cours naturel." The sensibility's activity is similar to its normal activity, though more intense, but its orientation, so to speak, is different. The whole being of the reader is concentrated on the poem, and the sensibility functions within a certain framework imposed by the poem. This "phase" constituted by the reading of the poem is seen by Valéry as

une certaine tension ou exaltation ... un *monde* ... ou un *mode d'existence* tout harmonique.[2]

Everything contributes to set in motion a certain very special internal organization—

l'être qui vit de rythmes, de contrastes, de symétries, de similitudes.[3]

The "phase" is in a state of perpetual change, according to the different selves which are in process of being created and then disappearing, according to the particular variability of the reader's mind and sensibility. The selves which are created and destroyed

---

significations et d'associations d'un mot." Cf. also *Cahiers, tome sixième*, p. 343: "L'ambiguïté est le (domaine) propre de la poésie. Tout vers est équivoque, plurivoque—comme sa structure, sound + sense—l'indique."

[1] *Poésie et pensée abstraite, Var. V*, p. 158.
[2] *Au sujet du Cimetière Marin, Var. III*, p. 63.
[3] *Esquisse d'un éloge de la virtuosité*, p. III.

s'éveillent ou s'émeuvent en chacun par les différences et les concordances, les consonances ou les dissonances qui se déclarent de proche en proche entre ce qui est lu, et ce qui était secrètement attendu.[1]

The words of the poem give the variations in sensation which affect the "internité." But, though they can influence, they can hardly control completely the sensations which travel along the path traced by Valéry from the "moi instantané" to the complete self. These developments depend largely on the particular and individual nature of the reader. Valéry acknowledges this, and thinks that the poet can gain thereby. Provided that the intellect's classifying function is controlled, the individual developments actually help to make the impressions received from the poem more profound and resonant. The "implexe" of the reader becomes involved. The richer and more varied it is, the more the reader will be stimulated and the more numerous will be the interactions of the various parts of the "internité"—exactly what is needed to achieve the "aesthetic infinite." The enjoyment to be got from the poem depends partly on what the reader *can* feel or learn. The relationship is a delicate one between what the poet can demand in effort from his reader and what the reader can and will contribute himself during the reading of the poem. We remember the well-known distinction which Valéry often drew between those poets who are created by their public and those who create their own public.[2] Valéry, of course, favours the latter type, and says explicitly that the poet can

> transformer le consommateur en producteur par voie de difficulté.[3]

Hence one may conclude that there must be a kind of struggle between the poem and the reader. The intellect automatically tries to classify; the "internité" tries to return to its "cours

---

[1] *Commentaire de Charmes, Var. III*, p. 72.
[2] Cf. *Choses tues, T.Q. I*, p. 18.
[3] *Cours de poétique* of 18 March 1938. This is another echo of Mallarmé.

naturel." A fine tension is created, and the effort of the intellect is very important; because it is unable to bring about its classifying act, it helps by its redoubled efforts in the communication of intense activity to the rest of "internité."

> L'effort excitant à l'effort. Tel est le nom de ce qui a fait toutes les grandes choses. Sudare jucunde.[1]

While this struggle and these efforts last—and they last as long as the "aesthetic infinite" lasts—the poem's effect becomes more and more compelling by virtue of its formal attractions. The reader soon has the poem by heart without realizing it. If the poem holds firm in the struggle—which must not be so great that the reader turns away disheartened—then the latter has to return to the poem when he wishes to renew the state of sensibility he has enjoyed. And in this manner, to quote Valéry's famous line,

> un beau vers renaît indéfiniment de ses cendres, il redevient, —comme l'effet de son effet,—cause harmonique de soi-même.[2]

While the "aesthetic infinite" lasts, the closed "worlds" of sensibility mentioned previously are excited simultaneously and interact with great complexity and intensity:

> Il se produit une sorte de liaison harmonique et réciproque entre nos impressions, nos idées, nos impulsions, nos moyens d'expression,—comme si toutes nos facultés devenaient tout à coup commensurables entre elles.[3]

—a kind of mystical and sublimating union is achieved. The expenditure of psychic energy involved is the real cause of our feeling of well-being as we read the poem. The agreement or disagreement of the various elements of our "internité"

---

[1] Mélange, p. 191. Cf. Cahiers, tome sixième, p. 450: "Le mérite d'un ouvrage est égal à l'effet produit (sur X) multiplié par la difficulté de l'obtenir (telle qu'elle apparaît à X)."

[2] Commentaire de Charmes, Var. III, p. 75.

[3] Autour de Corot, P.S.L., p. 148.

nous donne enfin toutes les modulations de la sensation de vivre, depuis le calme plat jusqu'à la tempête.[1]

*

We can now appreciate more fully, not merely the amount of technique implicit, for Valéry, in the poet's art, but also the background of his notion of 'attributed inspiration' as a value-judgement on the reader's part. His many remarks on the shock which the patiently organized poem has on the reader are too well known to need more than a reference:

> Telle œuvre, par exemple, est le fruit de longs soins, et elle assemble une quantité d'essais, de reprises, d'éliminations et de choix. Elle a demandé des mois et même des années de réflexion, et elle peut supposer aussi l'expérience et les acquisitions de toute une vie. Or l'effet de cette œuvre se déclarera en quelques instants . . . Il y a là une action de *démesure* . . . On obtient ainsi l'impression d'une puissance surhumaine.[2]

When the poet has written a successful poem, the grateful reader, ignorant (as he usually is) of the manner of composition, will sometimes conclude that the poem is so excellent that it must have been a divine communication; at the least, he will probably think that it was written during some quite exceptional state achieved by the poet, at a speed and with a high tension not far removed from the speed and tension of his own reading of the poem. Valéry has outlined this value-judgement many times:

> Un état qui ne peut se prolonger, qui nous met *hors* ou *loin*

---

[1] *Cours de poétique, Var. V*, p. 318. And, Valéry explains, "tout ceci, en dépensant, *à notre grand contentement*, notre propre énergie que [l'œuvre] évoque sur un mode si conforme au rendement le plus favorable de nos ressources organiques, que la sensation de l'effort se fait elle-même enivrante, et que nous nous sentons possesseurs pour être magnifiquement possédés" (*Ibid.*, pp. 317, 318).

[2] *Ibid.*, p. 306. Cf. *P.V.V.*, pp. 142, 143: "Mes poèmes me font l'effet d'une charge montée au sixième étage d'un édifice et qui retombe sur le lecteur non préparé, de son poids ainsi accru par l'élévation."

de nous-mêmes, et dans lequel l'*instable* pourtant nous soutient, tandis que le *stable* n'y figure que par accident, nous donne l'idée d'une existence toute capable des moments les plus rares de la nôtre, toute composée des *valeurs-limites* de nos facultés. Je songe à ce qu'on nomme vulgairement: *inspiration.*[1]

His view that inspiration is a myth must be linked with his belief in the mythopœic tendency of most human beings. He seems to think that for most readers, who, unlike himself, are not interested in the means and the functioning of art and the artist, so much as in the enjoyment of the poetic expression, "le plaisir ingénu de *croire*" is indispensable, for it engenders "le plaisir ingénu de produire, et . . . supporte toute lecture." [2] The reader lives with, and to some extent on, myths. The poet profits from the energy and euphoria occasioned by these myths.[3] If the reader knew that a given work which appeared to him as inspired had in fact been composed with much deliberation and lucidity regarding the effect it would have on him, then the poem would lose some of the transcendental value attached to the notion of inspired verse: the reaction of many readers would probably be that the poet is 'using' them, trifling with them. Much of the enjoyment of the poem would therefore be lost.

Valéry raised this problem on several occasions and always concluded that the poet was well advised to let the reader keep his myth of inspiration. Given the myth, and given Valéry's notion that the intellect must, for purposes of enjoyment, be

---

[1] *Degas, Danse, Dessin, P.S.L.*, p. 25. Cf. *Poésie et pensée abstraite, Var. V*, p. 156 and *La Création artistique, Vues*, p. 290.

[2] *Au sujet du Cimetière Marin, Var. III*, p. 60.

[3] Thus Valéry discusses the reaction of one reader: "Cet imbécile trouve que ce poème est (comme il dit) 'pessimiste'. Il ne sait pas un instant que si les vers s'étaient mieux tournés en les faisant joyeux, le poème eut été joyeux. Le noir fait mieux avec ces cheveux, dit le peintre.

"Mais il importe qu'une fois l'œuvre ainsi achevée, celui qui la contemple imagine des intentions. L'auteur fut dans son rôle à disposer du noir et du blanc sans scrupules. Le patient est dans le sien en interprétant—L'auteur n'a pas à *vouloir* ce qui n'est pas de son ressort" (*Cahiers, tome sixième*, p. 470).

prevented from working unhindered on the poem, one understands why he wrote that

l'artifice doit échapper au lecteur non prévenu, et l'effet ne pas révéler sa cause.[1]

The poet must not only achieve a state of "enchantement," he must also know how to conceal the means used to accomplish this.

Les hommes, pourraient-ils tolérer la poésie si elle ne se donnait pour une logomancie? [2]

It seems, he says, that the independence and mutual ignorance of poet and reader are almost essential for the poem to have a successful effect.[3] The points of view of poet and reader are incompatible, since the poem is, for the poet, the end, for the reader, the beginning, of developments each of which can be quite separate from the other.[4] This does not contradict the theories concerning technique already given, which implied the considerable control exercised by the poet over the poem and the reader. This control is, so to speak, general, ensuring the state of "enchantement" and the curb on the intellect's classifying function. Thus Valéry lists in his lecture on *la création artistique* the difficulties of the poet: during his search for infallible precision in the effects he wishes to produce on the reader, he encounters the inherent limitations of language,

---

[1] *Le Retour de Hollande, Var. II*, p. 37.   [2] *M.P.*, p. 196.

[3] *Cours de poétique, Var. V*, p. 307. Examining the importance of ambiguity, he explains in *Cahiers, tome sixième*, p. 118: "Le 'sens' d'un poème, comme celui d'un objet—est l'affaire du lecteur. Quantum potes, tantum aude.

"L'affaire du poète est de construire une sorte de corps verbal qui ait la solidité, mais l'ambiguïté, d'un objet. L'expérience montre qu'un poème trop simple (p. ex. abstrait) est *insuffisant* et s'use à la première vue. Ce n'est plus même un poème. Le pouvoir d'être repris et ressucé dépend du nombre d'interprétations compatibles avec le texte et ce nombre résulte lui-même d'une netteté qui impose l'obligation d'interpréter et d'une indétermination qui la repousse." (He refers to the clearness of the sound's attraction, of the melodic and harmonic effects, and the ambiguity of the sense).

[4] *Cours de poétique, Var. V*, p. 305.

such as its 'everyday' as well as its 'poetic' potential, or its imprecise conventions. He concludes that

> il n'y a donc guère que le rythme et les propriétés sensibles de la parole par quoi la littérature puisse atteindre l'être organique d'un lecteur avec quelque confiance dans la conformité de l'intention et des résultats.[1]

(The contrast is striking between this statement and Valéry's general, unqualified confidence as a young man in the poet's all-powerful technique). His considered view on this question, reiterated on several occasions, is linked with his notion of inspiration as a value-judgement by the reader:

> L'inspiration, mais c'est au lecteur qu'elle appartient et qu'elle

---

[1] La Création artistique, Vues, p. 291. Valéry spoke of the importance of what he called "le malentendu créateur" in the reader. This theme is clearly linked with his notion that inspiration is what the poet must create in the "consumer" and with his constant tendency to emphasize the gulf separating the latter and the poet. Jean Hytier (who discusses most lucidly these aspects of Valéry's thought, op. cit., pp. 235-252) points to the inherent opposition between two goals which attracted Valéry: a purely personal expression and a skilful subjugation of the reader's reactions. He remarks that it is not easy to reconcile the paradox of incommunicability with the subjugation of the reader (p. 240). Yet, in fact, Valéry does not usually so much argue that there must not be or cannot be communication between poet and reader as that the communication cannot or should not be *direct*. (Given his views on language, it is doubtful whether he believed that any communication could be truly direct). The poet, he thinks, obviously has intentions to convey; many of them, however, are not conveyed directly in that many readers, though affected by them, are not aware how the poet has achieved his effects. (The reader will often obtain more pleasure from the poem by misinterpreting the poet's intentions—see p. 90, note 3). The general control of which we have been speaking, involving Valéry's psychology of the reader, can be seen as an indirect communication of the poet's intentions. Discussing some of these points, Jean Hytier makes a happy distinction between "effets d'auteur" and "effets d'œuvre" (op. cit., p. 241), but seems to regard the latter (what Valéry would understand by indirect communication) as not being communication at all. Valéry seeks to control the impact of the "effets d'œuvre" as much as possible. There is inevitably considerable uncertainty governing them, but even this uncertainty, like that governing "le malentendu créateur," is to some extent allowed for and counted on.

est destinée, comme il appartient au poète d'y faire penser, d'y faire croire, de faire ce qu'il faut pour qu'on ne puisse attribuer qu'aux dieux un ouvrage trop parfait, ou trop émouvant pour sortir des mains incertaines de l'homme. L'objet même de l'art et le principe de ses artifices, il est précisément de communiquer l'impression d'un état idéal dans lequel l'homme qui l'obtiendrait serait capable de produire spontanément, sans effort, sans faiblesse, une ex-pression magnifique et merveilleusement ordonnée de sa nature et de nos destins.[1]

During the lecture he gave on *la création artistique*, Valéry was pressed by Monsieur Desjardins, who asked him point-blank whether he thought a poet could compose without "enthu-siasm." Valéry's reply (which, as our next chapter will show, was incomplete) could really have been predicted:

Je vous ai répondu d'avance en distinguant l'auteur du lecteur. Le poète dépend du lecteur. Je prétends même que l'inspiration est ce qu'il faut suggérer au lecteur. C'est au lecteur à fournir l'énergie.[2]

Thus, to study human psychology, even physiology, and their relationship to art, is an important part of the poet's technique, since the "consumer" has that which gives the poem life,

cette énergie humaine, ces forces intelligemment dirigées, que le constructeur avait prévues.[3]

Since Valéry considered the point of view of poet and reader incompatible, and desirably, fruitfully incompatible for the reasons indicated, it may seem strange that he wrote so much and so often on the theme of poetic creation. But he was too concerned with truth and too honest not to reveal his views: one could put it grandiloquently and say that Valéry-Teste, as

[1] *Propos sur la poésie, Conf.*, p. 85. See also *Cahiers, tome sixième*, pp. 287, 288.
[2] *La Création artistique, Vues*, p. 306.
[3] *Esquisse d'un éloge de la virtuosité*, p. IV. Cf. *Cahiers, tome quatrième*, p. 413: "Idéal littéraire—finir par savoir ne plus mettre sur sa page que du 'lecteur'."

opposed to Valéry the poet, had to speak his mind and took some pleasure in doing so if he shocked some mythopœic poetry-lovers. And in fact, Valéry's ideas concerning poetic creation were usually expressed in general terms, even when he was writing about a particular poem of his own. He did not reveal much of his detailed technique, the real tricks of the *métier* as he applied them. We are coming to know more of these tricks as manuscripts become available and as they are examined by perceptive critics.[1] We can distinguish between the generality of readers and what for want of a better term we would call Valéry's ideal reader. There is not a great gulf set between the point of view of this ideal reader and Valéry's own, as the creator of the poem. The ideal reader would naturally not be able to view a poem by Valéry as Valéry does, he would not know all the efforts and previous versions known to Valéry; but he would share with the poet his lack of illusion regarding the 'truth' of the poem, his pleasure in avoiding in the poem "les émotions immédiates de la vie," [2] "le désordre monotone de la vie extérieure." [3] Above all, he would either be indifferent to the question of inspiration or assume that the poet had had to work long and hard to create the verbal structure which gives both the poet and reader conscious delight in the exploitation of language and in the composite appeal to many elements in the "fonctionnement d'ensemble" indissociable from that very exploitation of language. Such an ideal reader would necessarily not believe in the common value-judgement inspiration, and his pleasure would probably be greater than those readers who do.[4]

[1] See the recent studies already mentioned, by L. J. Austin of *Le Cimetière Marin* and by Octave Nadal of *La Jeune Parque*.
[2] *Fragments des mémoires d'un poème, Var. V*, p. 90.   [3] *Ibid.*, p. 108.
[4] This conception of the ideal reader—inherent in Valéry's notion of "pure poetry"—is thus an important modification of his usual pronouncements on inspiration as a value-judgement by the reader.

CHAPTER IV

THE STAGES OF POETIC CREATION

W HEN Valéry writes about poetic creation, is he dealing with his own or what he considers to be all poets' inspiration or technique? In explanation of his position, it may be said that he is aware that other poets can write with a method very different from his own, especially those who, like poets loosely classed as romantics, rely on inspiration more than Valéry himself (even when allowance has been made for the differences between the theory and the practice of such poets). He believes that too much reliance on inspiration can result in good "fragments" of poetry, but that it also leads necessarily to patchiness, the worst of evils.[1] As we have seen, his ambition was to eliminate or reduce inspiration to a minimum, or at the least, to control it as effectively as possible. This ambition is implicit in his notion of "pure poetry."

He makes some trenchant remarks which seem to indicate that he believes certain stages have to be passed through by all poets, consciously or not. At other times, he stresses that he is speaking only of his own experience when he describes poetic composition. It is not easy to reconcile this contradiction, unless we conclude simply that he felt on occasion so convinced of the rightness of his ideas that he could not refrain from generalizing about *the* poetic experience. In the last analysis, his most constant attitude to this question is that he can only speak subjectively, but no man or poet can avoid this, even when he is discussing someone else. His view is that our idea of another poet's functioning is governed inevitably by the nature and limits of our own ego. In fact, it is obvious that Valéry's own experience is the point of departure for statements which, because they are often formulated impersonally and are not always prefaced by the remark that they are simply an explanation of one man's experience, take on the form of

[1] *Fragments des mémoires d'un poème, Var. V*, p. 100.

theories which, by implication, are applicable to other poets. This part of our study is based on Valéry's notion of stages in the poetic experience, as indicated by the following characteristic sentence:

> Je crois qu'il faut distinguer—quant à moi, je distingue excessivement,—les différents moments de la création de l'ouvrage, et je répète que ces moments d'espèces toutes diverses (et peut-être incomparables) sont nécessaires à toute production.[1]

These stages or moments we shall distinguish as: I Preparation: II Illumination: III Composition. There will be a further division, at a point occurring between the second and third stages, which we shall call "intimation" (translating Valéry's term, "attente"). These stages, corresponding to Valéry's own experience, are seen by Graham Wallas as roughly characteristic of all creative thought.[2] It is clear that, as Valéry points out, the several stages do or can mingle. What he did so often, and what we shall be doing, is to elucidate a continuous process.

STAGE I. PREPARATION

The first stage is essentially one of reflection and analysis, and not least, self-analysis. Valéry entered his so-called period of silence with the "mystique intellectuelle" we have examined. We must conceive this *mystique* as becoming something rather less mystical than in the early 1890s, but still mystical enough, a patient, determined search for precise formulations in the field of knowledge and self-knowledge. It is certain that he did not envisage this work principally as a period of preparation for the later years from 1913 to 1922, which brought forth

---

[1] *La Création artistique, Vues*, p. 306.
[2] Graham Wallas, *The Art of Thought*, London, C. A. Watts & Co. Ltd., 1945. This book has proved very useful. We acknowledge in particular our debt with regard to the two terms "illumination" and "intimation" which we have taken from Wallas.

such great poetry.[1] Knowledge about poetry and aesthetics represented but one corner of a wide field of knowledge which he worked with little or no thought of using his findings, and particularly of publishing them. When he did eventually, in 1913, for reasons which we shall examine later, return to poetic production, despite this partial change of direction in his life, he could still honestly describe *La Jeune Parque* as an "exercise" and claim that his interest was in the means rather than the end, and that

> le véritable bénéfice tiré par [lui] de cette *Parque*, réside dans des observations sur [lui]-même prises pendant le travail.[2]

When he emerged, from the 1920s onwards, as an aesthetician and theorist of poetry, he chose to stress what an important rôle this particular period of reflection and analysis had played in his own case, and what importance such a period, however different in nature and time, must play in the experience of most poets. Hence his praise of Poe and of the latter's ambition to find general laws in art and aesthetics, as much as in science and astronomy. Such laws are worth seeking for themselves, but also for the usefulness of possible applications of them. Praising Poe, Valéry is in fact praising himself as influenced by Poe (and others); he is confirming once again both the intrinsic and the practical value of his early conception of genius as the mind which, by analysis, finds relationships or *lois de continuité* governing apparently heterogeneous phenomena. He stresses, however, that such researches are most valuable when they have been pursued for their intrinsic worth with no regard for practical consequences:

> On ne revient à la pratique qu'après un éloignement si sévère qu'il semble infini, pendant lequel il faut être comme

---

[1] Cf. *La Création artistique, Vues*, p. 291: "De 1892 à 1912, je n'ai travaillé que pour moi-même, sans aucune idée de publication. Ma carrière littéraire s'est déclarée fort tard et fut déterminée par des circonstances indépendantes de ma volonté."

[2] *L.Q.*, pp. 123, 124.

aveugle et insensible aux craintes des conséquences que l'on tire, pour ne s'attacher qu'à leur rigueur. La pratique qui doit *juger* enfin, ne doit pas avoir commandé.[1]

The autobiographical and self-confirming nature of this statement is obvious. It is interesting to note how the principle enunciated is corroborated by many of those who speak with knowledge of many kinds of research.

He thus attaches great importance to this period of preparation, of self-preparation, speaking with enthusiasm of

l'intervention de la *méditation théorique*, c'est-à-dire d'une analyse aussi serrée, aussi pénétrante que l'on voudra, usant même des ressources d'un symbolisme abstrait, de notations organisées, en somme, de tous les moyens de l'esprit scientifique appliqués à un ordre de faits qui semblent au premier regard n'exister que dans le domaine de la vie affective et intuitive.[2]

What advantages accrue from this reflection? The poet can acquire sound notions about the nature of language and its particular form in literature and poetry, and about the functioning of the reader and the poet himself. Theorizing characterizes particularly the stage we have called preparation, but it is not to be thought of as being confined exclusively to this stage. Valéry does not claim merely that such thought helps in the production of poetry; he suggests also that

l'emploi des facultés abstraites,—d'une sorte de calcul conscient,—puisse non seulement s'accorder avec l'exercice d'un art,—c'est-à-dire avec la production ou création de valeurs poétiques,—mais encore soit indispensable pour porter à un degré suprême d'efficacité et de puissance l'action de l'artiste et la portée de l'œuvre.[3]

It is again obvious that this generalization is indissociable from his own experience and his own ideal of poetry. Another

---

[1] *Ibid.*, p. 142.   [2] *La Création artistique, Vues*, p. 289.   [3] *Ibid.*

advantage is that, thanks to an increase in self-knowledge and self-control, the poet can discover his limitations and work within them:

> ce que l'esprit peut faire de plus efficace, c'est . . . d'entrevoir ses liaisons profondes—et en somme—ses limites vraies. Notre maîtrise coïncide avec la connaissance de nos limites.[1]

To know oneself really well is, he thinks, to be on the threshold of original creation:

> *Inventer, ce n'est que se comprendre.* On a l'idée d'un appareil réversible comme téléphone, ou dynamo.[2]

Such perfect co-ordination is never, of course, actually obtained in life, but it remains an ideal to be striven towards; having such a goal enables a partial degree of success to be achieved. A final advantage of such consciousness and abstraction, one which he eloquently extolled, is that the poet can at a certain stage create from preoccupations with form; what he finds he can do with language will be the guiding principle of what he actually does. The finding of an idea from a rhyme is a good instance.

> Il en est chez qui le développement des moyens devient si avancé, et d'ailleurs si bien identifié à leur intelligence, qu'ils parviennent à 'penser', à 'inventer' dans le monde de l'exécution, à partir des moyens mêmes. La musique déduite des propriétés des sons; l'architecture déduite de la matière et des forces; la littérature, de la possession du langage et de son rôle singulier et de ses modifications,—en un mot, la partie réelle des arts excitant leur partie imaginaire, l'acte possible créant son objet, ce que je puis m'éclairant ce que je veux, et m'offrant des dessins à la fois tout inattendus et tout réalisables . . .[3]

---

[1] Lair–Dubreuil et Andrieux, *Catalogue de la bibliothèque de P. Souday,* p. 143.
[2] *Calepin d'un poète, Poésies,* p. 184.
[3] *Je disais quelquefois à Stéphane Mallarmé, Mall.,* p. 57.

Above all, this devotion to analysis, because it makes the poet more independent with regard to language, more master of his thoughts,[1] enables him to exercise the supreme prerogative of analytical thought, namely, to provoke, to discover and to examine the greatest possible variety of combinations and solutions. This, thinks Valéry, can bring nothing but good to the poet in search of perfection.

*

Elucidating the essential nature of the poet transforms the poet who has performed the task. Valéry analyses the "tempérament poétique essentiel," [2] by which he means those qualities which are present in the person capable of having the "poetic state" or "poetic emotion." The "tempérament poétique essentiel," according to him, does not necessarily lead the possessor of it to have verbal "fragments" or to compose poems, and, therefore, it may belong in varying degrees to quite a large number of people, who nevertheless constitute a small minority of the human race. It may also be such that at certain periods of the possessor's life it is merely dormant, in that no "poetic state" arises at all. Valéry thinks that the person with a poetic temperament is not distinguished so much by the intensity of his emotions as by his ability to be moved by things which do not move the majority of people. Such persons are, so to speak, "résonateurs," magnifying for pleasurably artistic purposes reactions which are not so magnified by ordinary men.[3] They are to be recognized by

> leur faculté de s'émouvoir excessivement de choses qui n'émeuvent personne, et par leur faculté de se donner à eux-mêmes une foule de passions, d'états admirables et de sentiments vifs auxquels suffit le moindre prétexte pour naître du néant et s'exalter. Ils possèdent, en quelque sorte, en soi-mêmes, infiniment plus de réponses que la vie ordi-

---

[1] *Propos*, p. 49.   [2] *Poésie, préambule*, p. XIV.
[3] Cf. *Cahiers, tome sixième*, p. 448: "La fécondité relative de tel esprit n'est que son aptitude ou acquise ou originelle à ne pas laisser perdre mille incidents mentaux qui ne sont pas retenus chez les autres."

naire n'a de questions à leur proposer; et ceci leur est cette richesse toujours imminente, surabondante et comme irritable qui développe des trésors, et même des mondes, pour un rien.

And he adds:

Cette grandeur des effets auprès de cette petitesse des causes, voilà ce qui distingue le tempérament poétique essentiel.[1]

A picture thus emerges of the person with a poetic temperament as a creature who has more selves, more "possibilité" than the average man. His sensibility receives more impulsions which are the origin of a richer and more powerful development in his "fonctionnement d'ensemble." Valéry conceives of the "tempérament poétique essenticl" as innate; without it, "poetic states" will not be experienced. All those who do have it are potential pocts if they have or develop other gifts or qualities as well—a certain feeling for language, a certain ability to handle it, in short, if they acquire the *métier* of poetic composition. This potential poetic temperament reveals itself in

le plaisir à éprouver à être seul avec soi-même, à trouver en soi-même l'intérêt peut-être factice, peut-être exagéré, en tout cas un intérêt puissant . . . Peu à peu, il se fait le plaisir, que l'on recherche très volontiers, d'une vie secrète presque contemplative, d'une vie séparée, et cette vie conduit à un état qui, lui, est essentiel à la création du poète—car sur cet état pourra venir se greffer cette sorte de métier à acquérir . . .[2]

Many romantic poets would not have disavowed the major part of this definition. The essential difference of attitude between

---

[1] *Poésie, préambule*, p. XIV. Cf. *Cahiers, tome sixième*, p. 538: "Poète. L'homme — le comédien naturel dont le poète est l'exemplaire— Il est comme le prêtre du système nerveux total. Il en doit aux hommes l'exemple, l'image, la caricature, la transfigurée— "Depuis l'*idéal* de la sensibilité brute, fine jusqu'à l'*idéal* des coordinations et des actes les plus élevés."

[2] *Souvenirs poétiques*, pp. 17, 18.

the romantics and Valéry appears when Valéry clearly states that the contemplative self-regarding nature is a *sine qua non*, but not the most important element in the poet's constitution.

His mention of "cette sorte de métier à acquérir" confirms his well-known distinction between two aspects of the poet. 'Intermittent inspiration' is essential to the poet. It does not suffice to have 'intuitive inspiration' as well, for the latter gives only "fragments," verbal or rhythmical. These two forms of inspiration can be considered here as one aspect of the poet about which Valéry made statements with various nuances. At one stage in his youth, he believes that it is not necessary. His mature view generally reveals some distrust of this aspect, but concedes with varying tones of approval the necessity of it for poetic creation. A typical sentence of the later years reveals the attitude we have just described:

> L'art, à mes yeux, est un combat contre ce qui n'est pas. La spontanéité et le hasard heureux qui parfois nous habitent sont, sans doute, essentiels à toute création; ils offrent le prétexte et donnent l'impulsion. Mais toutes les puissances de l'homme doivent s'engager pour soutenir et établir ce qui vient de naître et qui tient à retomber dans le néant.[1]

The second aspect of the poet—his intelligence, his critical and evaluative faculties—is just as important as the first; it is more important, in that it could manage after a fashion alone:

> Il y a plus de bons vers faits froidement qu'il n'en est de chaudement faits; et plus de mauvais faits chaudement. On dirait que l'intelligence est plus capable de suppléer à la chaleur, que la chaleur à l'intelligence. Une machine peut marcher à faible pression, mais une pression sans machine n'entraîne rien.[2]

The function of the second aspect of the poet is to control and appraise:

---

[1] *De la ressemblance et de l'art, Vues*, pp. 332, 333.
[2] *Autres Rhumbs, T.Q. II*, p. 156.

Il faut être deux pour inventer—l'un forme des combinaisons, l'autre choisit, reconnaît ce qu'il désire et ce qu'on appelle 'génie' est bien moins l'acte de celui-là,—l'acte qui combine,—que la promptitude du second à comprendre la valeur de ce qui vient de se produire, et à saisir ce produit. (Le génie comme un jugement).[1]

As well as having this evaluative function, the second aspect of the poet organizes "le *tout* du poème"[2] which *is* the poem for Valéry. He argues that the evaluative and co-ordinating faculty is implicit in the simplest and crudest poetry:

Il n'y aurait pas eu de poésie si le travail et les artifices ne permettaient, par l'essai d'une quantité de substitutions, de multiplier les coups heureux et d'assembler ce qu'il en faut pour composer une durée toute favorable.[3]

Valéry, we know, carried this tendency to its extreme limits. His aim is to write a poetry which will not just attempt in hit-or-miss fashion to play on the reader's sensibility, but which will bring about the participation of all his faculties in a complex, intense exaltation. To encompass his aim, the poet needs

l'attention, la modification du cours accidentel, naturel, instantané de la sensibilité; il nous faut pour cela obtenir cette modification intime qui va consister à juger des choses du haut de l'état de conscience plus complexe.[4]

When Valéry is comparing the poet with the average man, he chooses to distinguish and even oppose the two aspects or faculties just mentioned:

Un poète, en tant qu'architecte de poèmes, est donc assez différent de ce qu'il est comme producteur de ces éléments

[1] *Analecta, T.Q. II*, p. 234. Cf. *Fragments des mémoires d'un poème, Var. V*, p. 114 and *Note et Digression, Vinci*, pp. 23, 24.
[2] *Fontaines de mèmoire, P.S.L.* 1948, p. 248.
[3] *Variation sur une pensée annotée par l'auteur, Var. II*, pp. 42 and 44.
[4] *Cours de poétique* of 18 December 1938.

précieux dont toute poésie doit être composée, mais dont la composition se distingue, et exige un travail mental tout différent.[1]

His point of view is constantly and simply that the poet reacts more than ordinary men to the visitation of "poetic states" and, above all, wants to make something from them in words. But when he is talking of the poet alone, he stresses the interdependence of the two faculties:

C'est dans les questions de forme que l'intellect et la sensibilité doivent nécessairement se combiner. On n'écrit ni une fugue ni une symphonie sans calcul, et à mon avis le poème lui-même exige dans sa composition un exercice perpétuel de facultés de sentir et d'agir.[2]

And he adds the following comment:

D'ailleurs, la distinction 'intelligence-sensibilité', 'raison et inspiration' me paraît assez scolaire.

That may well be so, at least, without more careful qualification. The fact remains that he himself constantly made such a distinction even in his advanced years, during his *cours de poétique*. Taking a comprehensive view, however, it is clear that his ideas have changed radically since his youth—as our last quotation (from a letter of 1941) reveals. It is no longer a question of opposing composition based entirely on technique to composition based entirely on 'total inspiration', but a wise awareness of the essential interdependence of two elements. The older he got, the more Valéry moved in this direction, so that he wrote three years before his death, in 1942, when speaking of Servien's poems, that

il ne peut s'agir des deux 'esprits' baptisés par Pascal, s'ignorant dans le même homme qu'ils habitent. C'est au contraire parce qu'ils se connaissent en profondeur qu'ils

---

[1] *Poésie et pensée abstraite, Var. V*, pp. 158, 159.   [2] *L.Q.*, p. 234.

peuvent si heureusement s'exercer à produire, en regard l'un de l'autre, des fruits très différents et très précieux.[1]

He blamed the romantics for establishing, or at least for popularizing, an opposition between the two faculties:

> L'idée niaise et funeste d'opposer la connaissance approfondie des moyens d'exécution, l'observance des préceptes éprouvés, le travail savamment soutenu, toujours mené *par ordre* à son terme (et ce terme de perfection soustrait à la fantaisie individuelle)—à l'acte impulsif de la sensibilité singulière, est un des traits les plus certains et les plus déplorables de la légèreté et de la faiblesse de caractère qui ont marqué l'âge romantique.[2]

The brunt of his accusation seems in fact to be that the romantics chose to exaggerate the importance of the wrong element in the dichotomy. He would probably not have been so scathing if, like him, they had emphasized the primacy of intelligence rather than sensibility. However, his mature view, his final view, chronologically speaking, is that he is

> celui qui n'oppose jamais, qui ne sait pas opposer, l'intelligence à la sensibilité, la conscience réfléchie à ses données immédiates.[3]

But let us be clear that he means this, as far as art or the composition of poetry is concerned.[4]

---

[1] *Le Cas Servien*, in *Orient* by P. Servien, Dijon, Gallimard, 1942, pp. 90, 91.

[2] *Autour de Corot*, P.S.L., p. 154.

[3] *Philosophie de la danse*, *Conf.*, p. 180.

[4] Cf. the views expressed by Sir Maurice Bowra (influenced by Valéry?): "Above all, he [the poet] must use his intelligence, not merely for criticism, but as an actual instrument in composition... It is sometimes assumed that inspiration is irrational, defies or dodges the critical intelligence, and has no truck with hard thought. But in the greatest works of man the active mind has always played a prominent part... Modern attempts to divorce poetry from reason seem doomed to failure, because it is an essential part of the human consciousness, it is the whole of this consciousness, not merely this or that part of it, which inspiration sets to work" (*Inspiration and Poetry* [Rede lecture delivered at Cambridge in 1951], London, Macmillan, 1955, p. 24).

Yet, in fact, Valéry does often envisage intellect and sensibility as separate elements working the one against the other. Thus he writes of

la condition contrariée de l'état artiste. Il doit observer comme s'il ignorait tout et il doit exécuter comme s'il savait tout. Aucune connaissance dans la sensation, mais aucune ignorance dans la transformation.[1]

The aphorism reveals a preoccupation with habit, a frequent theme in his writings. His warnings on this subject are well known. They are epitomized for all the world to see in the engraving on the *Palais de Chaillot*:

Regarder comme jamais vues toutes choses qui sont au monde.[2]

Before a given object or situation, the average man's sensibility, instead of receiving a kind of shock constituted by a really new impression, quickly returns to the "cours naturel" by the force of habit and because of his myths or the "mental sets" implicit in his utilitarian viewpoint.[3] Valéry believes that the poet has to work against the force of habit, controlling the element of meaning in the impressions he receives, "pour revenir à la valeur sensorielle." [4] He must seek as deliberately as possible to control, enrich and sharpen his sensibility. It is

[1] *M.P.*, p. 39.

[2] Cf. *Pour un portrait de Monsieur Teste, Teste II*, p. 117: "La notion de choses extérieures est une restriction des combinaisons. L'imagination significative est une tricherie affective."

[3] Cf. *Cahiers, tome huitième*, p. 352: "L'habitude n'est pas suppression de la sensibilité mais des réactions qui en procèdent, et qui d'ailleurs la renforcent.

"D'autre part l'habitude s'accompagne d'une spécialisation. c à d.: au début —la situation ou l'excitation A *intéresse, parcourt*, un domaine dans l'être, mal déterminé.

"Peu à peu, si l'A se répète, le trajet se réduit à ce qui suffit pour annuler au plus tôt la perturbation... Ce *trajet tend à coïncider avec le cours naturel*... L'habitude tend à faire de l'acte ou de la réaction—ou de la non réaction— la *propriété* d'une excitation minima."

[4] *Cours de poétique* of 26 March 1938.

in this way that the poet can incorporate into his poem the new impressions, however stylised, which will help to create the poetic world and the "entretien de sensibilité" which a poem essentially is for Valéry. The artist or the poet

> répond à l'habitude par l'insolite, perçoit ce qu'il y a d'étrange dans le banal, distille le pur de l'impur . . . [Ses] démons jouent à déjouer le principe de la dégradation des sensations par l'habitude.[1]

The programme to be followed by the poet stems from Valéry's general attitude regarding language. He thinks that for most people, most of the time, its function is

> de nous faire repasser *au voisinage* d'états déjà éprouvés, de régulariser, ou d'instituer, la répétition.[2]

The poet should "penser le plus possible de l'automatisme verbal."[3] He can deliberately cultivate free association for poetic purposes, with his intelligence ever watching for what it can discover and use. Valéry's image of himself as the spider at the centre of a web of ideas and feelings in fairly free association shows how he practises what he preaches. We can thus see how he adumbrates a *construction du poète*. The poet multiplies further the initial multiplicity of self.[4] By reliance on 'awareness', the "moi pur," which Valéry defined as "un refus indéfini d'être quoi que ce soit,"[5] the poet can attempt to strip himself of all but the "moi instantané" for a short time in order to increase, later, the novelty and diversity of his impressions. Such seems to be the theory. It is difficult to assess the extent to which he was able to put it into practice. He himself is the first to stress the inherent difficulty of doing so. At the least, the theory remains an ideal to be striven towards and once again we must remark that having such an ideal

---

[1] *Au sujet de Berthe Morisot, Vues*, p. 337.
[2] *Léonard et les philosophes, Vinci*, p. 158.   [3] *Ibid.*
[4] Cf. *Histoires brisées*, p. 156: "Je suis celui que je suis à chaque instant."
[5] *Note et Digression, Vinci*, p. 46.

transforms the poet and enables a partial degree of success to be achieved.

The stage of preparation not only precedes the composition of a given poem: it also occurs during composition. Ideally, it is seen as coming before the composition of a poet's *best* poems. Valéry referred frequently to this preparation of the "field of possibilities" [1] constituted by the poet's psyche, usually in the metaphorical terms of soil and growth:

> L'étendue et la richesse de cette production [de sensibilité] dépend uniquement . . . de la richesse du sol dans lequel le germe se place. Plus l'homme est savant, plus cette production est abondante, plus elle est précise, plus elle est instante, plus est elle puissante.[2]

His notion is simply that, given this truth, the poet can to a certain extent profit from it by consciously preparing the self so that the "poetic state" will provide the germ ('intuitive inspiration'—verbal or rhythmical illumination) and also so that the illumination will, so to speak, take root and lead to developments useful for poetic production.

There will be no guarantee that this preparation will always produce worth-while results, but, unlike his youthful self, Valéry is content with a *calcul des probabilités*. The significance

[1] *Cours de poétique* of 11 March 1938.

[2] *Cours de poétique* of 18 December 1937. The same point is made by Rosamond Harding in her *Anatomy of Inspiration*, supported by quotations from George Eliot, Daudet and Sibelius, and by J. E. Downey in her *Creative Imagination*. Downey comes to exactly the same conclusions as Valéry: "We would emphasize as important the fact that creative intelligence is no special prerogative of the poet or novelist or artist. All adults can cite instances of lucky guesses, sudden insights, unexpected generalizations, surprising bits of repartee that amazed them as much as the individual to whom addressed. The point, however, should be stressed that all so-called inspirations occur strictly within the limit of the individual's capacity, training and previous cogitations. It was to Hamilton, the mathematician, and not to Byron, the poet, that the famous discovery of the quaternions came. 'Kubla Khan' was dreamed by Coleridge; the Benzene Theory, by Kebulé, the chemist. Inspiration may be a flash-up from the unconscious but it is no chance explosion occurring indifferently in feeble-minded or genius" (*op. cit.*, p. 158).

he attaches to the point is indicated by his references to it in his important lecture on *la création artistique*:

> Le fait nouveau qui se produit à notre esprit dépend d'une certaine sensibilité momentanée dont on ne peut dire si elle le saisit ou si elle le provoque. Tel état, telle orientation des recherches la modifient. Je songe au phénomène de la sensibilisation qui se voit en biologie . . . et je me demande si l'effet du travail intellectuel n'est pas de favoriser je ne sais quel accroissement de sensibilité? Le travail ne conduirait pas à la solution (dans l'ordre esthétique, d'ailleurs, ni les problèmes ni les solutions ne sont en général déterminés), mais il multiplierait les chances favorables au dessein général de l'artiste; il ferait momentanément de l'artiste un résonateur très sensible à tous les incidents de conscience qui peuvent servir son dessein.[1]

The poet's aim during the stage of preparation is to learn as much as possible about other fields of knowledge, other patterns of reality, to use all his faculties and to know himself. The universal mind symbolized by the da Vinci of the *Introduction* still remains, however modified, an ideal for Valéry, so that in 1942, as in 1895, he praises him for being able to view reality, to exist, in different ways: da Vinci

> pouvait regarder le même spectacle ou le même objet, tantôt comme l'eût regardé un peintre, et tantôt en naturaliste; tantôt comme un physicien, et d'autres fois comme un poète; et aucun de ces regards n'était superficiel.[2]

The theories of the mature Valéry link with those of the Valéry of 1895 and with the nascent realizations of the young man of 1890, who wrote to Pierre Louÿs:

> A dire vrai, je crois plus que jamais que je suis plusieurs.[3]

---

[1] *La Création artistique, Vues*, p. 305.
[2] Valéry's preface to *Les Carnets de Léonard de Vinci*, Paris, Gallimard, 1942, p. 7.
[3] *L.Q.*, p. 18. Cf. his reference to "la condition générale des poètes, qui est de posséder plusieurs existences" (in his preface to *Coffrets Etoilés*, by A. Lebey, Paris, La Connaissance du Livre, 1918, p. V).

The stage of preparation can be seen as taking place on two levels or in two ways. On the first level, the poet prepares himself by non-specialization. Valéry states quite clearly:

> je n'ai pas consacré mon long temps de silence à l'étude de la technique du vers. Je n'ai guère plus songé au vers pendant ce retrait.[1]

He goes on to point out how this period of non-specialization contributed to his poetic achievement:

> le temps, les 23 ans et plus dépensés à maintes analyses, les transformations intérieures créées ou adoptées à leur intention, n'ont pas peu contribué, quand je suis revenu à la poésie, à m'en faire pénétrer certaines finesses. J'ai employé, si vous supportez cette image, des appareils cent et mille fois plus précis à observer *la même chose* que j'observais en 1891. Le degré de précision transforme une question, et, parfois, une 4e décimale change toute l'idée que l'on avait jusqu'avant elle du monde.[2]

On the second level, it is a question of specialization in the particular *métier*, poetry. He so specialized from 1913 onwards, taking up threads he had laid aside in the 1890s.

Valéry explained frequently and eloquently how desirable and yet how difficult it is to profit from the method of preparation we have outlined; there is difficulty in pursuing the method to make discoveries, even greater difficulty in making use of the discoveries. The only satisfactory goal is that of the method made flesh, the discoveries having become an integral part of the poet's being. The poet has to exert himself for a long time to *be* what his analytical mind has discovered. Much practice is essential—both in non-specialized study and in poetic expression. He has expressed this problem in various aphorisms:

> Il n'y a qu'une chose à faire: se refaire. Ce n'est pas simple.[3]

---

[1] *L.Q.*, p. 131.   [2] *Ibid.*, pp. 131, 132.   [3] *M.P.*, p. 166.

Trouver n'est rien. Le difficile est de s'ajouter ce qu'on trouve.[1]

Il faut tant d'années pour que les vérités que l'on s'est faites deviennent notre chair même.[2]

The time-lag is inevitable.[3]

Valéry is thus led, as a kind of climax to the above consider-ations, to his view that "l'œuvre capitale d'un artiste, c'est l'artiste lui-même." [4] If we could perform the impossible and witness the struggles of the artist,

> alors l'existence d'un artiste nous apparaîtrait, sans doute, comme une longue et constante préparation de quelque état suprême : nous assisterions à la construction d'un créateur . . . l'artiste, donc, œuvre capitale, œuvre unique et secrète de soi-même se façonne et se modèle peu à peu, se déchiffre et se reconnaît; il devient un homme nouveau, *celui qui fait enfin ce que lui seul peut faire.*[5]

What would seem to be inspiration to an onlooker is thus seen as a point of arrival and not a point of departure.[6] Valéry called it "improvisation de degré supérieur," [7] that supreme state in which

> esprit de finesse, esprit de géométrie, on les épouse, on les abandonne, comme fait le cheval accompli ses rythmes

[1] *La Soirée avec Monsieur Teste, Teste*, p. 28.

[2] *Note et Digression, Vinci*, p. 22.

[3] Cf. *Lettre à Madariaga, Vues*, p. 106: "La lenteur d'évolution, la résistance instinctive à l'inconnu, sont les lois de fond des êtres, même de ceux dont l'intelligence est la plus vive."

[4] *Discours à l'inauguration du monument élevé à la mémoire d'Emile Verhaeren à Paris*, p. 9.

[5] *Ibid.*

[6] Cf. *Cahiers, tome sixième*, p. 65: "Le travail psychique non désordonné consiste, en gros, dans une suite de tâtonnements qui cherchent à construire l'appareil instantané, le moment, l'état—dont l'acte unique serait enfin la production d'un certain résultat désiré.
"On n'a pas assez remarqué ce double degré. Ce travail s'applique non directement a produire la chose, mais à produire ce qui produira la chose."

[7] *Autour de Corot, P.S.L.*, p. 147.

successifs ... Il doit suffire à l'être suprêmement coordonné de se prescrire certaines modifications cachées et très simples au regard de la volonté, et immédiatement il passe de l'ordre des transformations purement formelles et des actes symboliques au régime de la connaissance imparfaite et des réalités spontanées.[1]

Mallarmé is seen by Valéry as the poet of poets precisely because he reached this high peak of achievement:

il avait laborieusement dominé, modifié, approfondi le poète semblable aux autres qu'il était né. Il avait recherché, reconnu les principes du désir qui engendre l'acte poétique; défini, isolé son élément pur,—et il s'était fait *le virtuose de cette discipline de pureté*,—l'être qui s'étudie à jouer infailliblement du plus rare de soi.[2]

The "improvisation de degré supérieur" can be considered as a form of 'exalted inspiration', growing ever stronger and surer of itself. When he takes up this theme, a certain almost lyrical note usually shows itself, and we are made aware how the *mystique* of the young Valéry can still shine forth, if not as a dream of universal knowledge, at least as a dream of power through thought and self-control exercised during poetic creation.[3] The *poetry* of creation is one of his major themes:

---

[1] *Note et Digression, Vinci*, p. 28.
[2] *Je disais quelquefois à Stéphane Mallarmé, Mall.*, p. 55. It is with such considerations in mind that Valéry affirms: "Le 'genie' est une habitude que prennent certains" (*Cahiers, tome quatrième*, p. 394). Cf. also in the same *cahier*, p. 778: "Les trouvailles, chez qui trouve assez souvent—*deviennent* résultat d'une opération à peu près sûre, et quoiqu'elle ne se fasse toute consciente, elle est bien déterminée, attachée à une attitude.
"L'exception se fait habitude, s'apprivoise."
[3] Cf. *Cahiers, tome cinquième*, p. 285: "Je distingue par le mot de *Possession*, l'état le plus élevé, le plus enviable de l'être. Quand il est entièrement imminent, les fonctions essentielles tout effacées; tout gonfé d'énergie disponible, bien répartie entre les extenseurs et les modérateurs; capable d'agir aussi promptement, aussi lentement qu'il voudra; ayant la double propriété de l'explosif et du réversible; doué d'élasticité; de transparence; apte aux

Le spontané est le fruit d'une conquête. Il n'appartient qu'à ceux qui ont acquis la certitude de pouvoir conduire un travail à l'extrême de l'exécution, d'en conserver l'unité de l'ensemble en réalisant les parties et sans perdre en chemin l'esprit ni la nature.—Il n'arrive qu'à eux, quelque jour, dans quelque occasion, le bonheur de surprendre, définir, en quelques notes, en quelques traits, *l'être d'une impression*. Ils montrent à la fois, dans ce peu de substance sonore ou graphique, l'émotion d'un instant et la profondeur d'une science qui a coûté toute une vie. Ils jouissent enfin de s'être faits instruments de leurs suprêmes découvertes, et ils peuvent à présent improviser en pleine possession de leur puissance.[1]

When writing about this inspired improvisation in his maturity, Valéry uses words and betrays an intensity of feeling which constitute a real reinstatement of the notion of inspiration, in all our senses save the first. The following analyses contradict views expressed in 1889 and are substantially different from many remarks disparaging inspiration made after 1920:

Entre les intentions et les moyens, entre les conceptions du *fond* et les actions qui engendrent la *forme*, il n'y a plus de contraste. Entre la pensée de l'artiste et la manière de son art, s'est instituée une certaine correspondance, remarquable par une réciprocité dont ceux qui ne l'ont pas éprouvée ne peuvent imaginer l'existence[2]—(text first published in 1932).

---

solutions finies—bon pour suivre un contour, comme pour trancher. Tous ses souvenirs garnissant bien un carquois.

"C'est ce magnifique état que l'on assimile à un état d'équilibre et que l'on cherche à reconquérer, a maintenir, à nourrir indéfiniment. Etat du plus grand luxe physique et psychologique." But it is not only during poetic creation that this state is experienced by Valéry.

[1] *Autour de Corot, P.S.L.*, p. 146. Sir Maurice Bowra makes the same point about the poet: "All his labours to fashion a style, to decide what kind of poetry he should write, are suddenly rewarded by what looks like an effortless success, since in it he feels no strain or hesitation or uncertainty" (*op. cit.*, p. 21).

[2] *Autour de Corot, P.S.L.*, p. 147.

Chez le grand artiste, la sensibilité et les moyens sont dans une relation particulièrement intime et *réciproque* qui, dans l'état vulgairement connu sous le nom d'*inspiration*, en arrive à une sorte de jouissance, échange ou correspondance presque parfaite entre le désir et ce qui le comble, le vouloir et le pouvoir, l'idée et l'acte, jusqu'au point de résolution où cesse cet excès d'unité composée, où l'être exceptionnel qui s'était constitué de nos sens, de nos forces, de nos idéaux, de nos trésors acquis, se disloque, se défait, nous abandonne à notre commerce de *minutes sans valeur* contre *perceptions sans avenir*, laissant après soi quelque *fragment* qui ne peut avoir été obtenu que dans un *temps*, ou dans un *monde*, ou sous une *pression*, ou grâce à une *température* de l'âme très différents de ceux qui contiennent ou produisent du *N'importe Quoi* . . . ([1]—text first published in 1938).

This reinstatement of the notion of inspiration is expressed elsewhere with similar inspirational terminology:

Chaque esprit peut se regarder comme un laboratoire naturel où des traitements particuliers s'appliquent à transformer une substance générale. Les produits des uns étonnent les autres. Celui-ci obtient du diamant, à partir du carbone commun, sous des pressions et des températures inconnues aux autres. On l'analyse. Ce n'est que du carbone, dit-on. Mais on ne sait pas le reproduire ([2]—text first published in 1942).

Speaking of P. Servien's poems, Valéry describes 'exalted inspiration'—in the form, it seems, of "improvisation de degré supérieur"—by turning to a less colourful and less metaphorical description of this special state of the poet:

Ces arrangements de syllabes ne peuvent se produire que dans un état privilégié qui a ses contraintes et ses libertés propres, très différentes des possibilités ordinaires ([3]—text first published in 1942).

[1] *Degas, Danse, Dessin, P.S.L.*, p. 55.   [2] *M.P.*, pp. 165, 166.
[3] *Le Cas Servien*, in *Orient*, by P. Servien, Dijon, Gallimard, 1942, p. 97.

Discussing the poems of Ladislas Mécs, he uses yet another image to convey essentially the same notion: he reflects on

[les] propriétés paradoxales qu'acquiert un corps en rotation rapide: une toupie tient sur sa pointe, se redresse, semble réagir aux chocs comme un être vivant, et les forces qui agissent sur elle la trouvent tout autre qu'au repos. Ne sont-ce pas des propriétés paradoxales qu'acquiert la pensée, et plus exactement, la faculté du langage chez le poète, quand l'exaltation lyrique s'empare de lui? ([1]—text first published in 1944).

When we consider these statements, it is ironical to reflect that many readers can only too well imagine that a state of inspiration can exist, but do not realize that it is a "conquest" and not a free gift, that great preparation and training were essential to achieve it. Valéry is careful to stress that the state of inspired improvisation is a "unité composée," an "être exceptionnel." One imagines that the poet has to rise slowly to this state, if he can, each time he seeks to compose. And then, most important of all, Valéry stresses that this state can usually give birth only to a "fragment":

Je dis un *fragment* . . . car il y a peu de chances pour que ces unions assez brèves nous livrent *toute* une œuvre de quelque étendue. C'est qu'interviennent le savoir, la durée, la reprise, les jugements. Il faut une bonne tête pour exploiter les bonheurs, maîtriser les trouvailles, et *finir*.[2]

In other words, while admitting and describing in quite eloquent language 'exalted inspiration' (which implies 'inter-

---

[1] Valéry's preface to the *Poèmes* of L. Mécs, Paris, Horizons de France, 1944, p. XVII. Cf. *Cahiers, tome sixième*, p. 414: "Dans l'état 'd'inspiration' les éléments de la pensée semblent obéir à une 'physique' sensiblement différente de celle ordinaire. Les mêmes mots et actes sont soumis à d'autres lois, capables d'autres combinaisons.

"De même les corps en mouvement de rotation n'ont pas la même mécanique que les corps simplement en translation. Conséquences pour l'équilibre, les chocs,—etc. La *valence* des mots change dans ces états."

[2] *Degas, Danse, Dessin, P.S.L.*, p. 55.

mittent' and 'intuitive inspiration' as well), he still rejects 'total inspiration'.

Valéry referred to the ease with which he wrote certain poems of *Charmes*. It seems fairly obvious that *Charmes* would have been in any case a less arduous task of composition than *La Jeune Parque*, but it is also true that he experienced the benefit of "improvisation de degré supérieur" because his 'hand was in' after he had spent so long over his longest poem:

> Alors, ayant achevé ma *Jeune Parque*, il m'est arrivé, quelques semaines après, d'écrire en très peu de temps, très rapidement, *Aurore* et *Palme*, et j'ai eu l'impression moi-même qu'ayant fait de l'escrime avec une barre de plomb j'en faisais avec un fleuret. Je me sentais en possession d'une liberté durement acquise dans le métier de faire des vers.[1]

*

In conclusion, one could speak of this period or stage of preparation, as Graham Wallas does, in terms of "incubation." Thus, when Valéry was rather unenthusiastically glancing at the copy of the poems written in his youth which Gide and Gallimard had given him,

> l'inégalité dans un ouvrage [lui] apparut alors, tout à coup, le pire des maux...[2]

The idea struck him very forcibly, then subsided, a seed destined to grow in the following manner:

> Cette remarque [he notes] fut un germe. Elle ne fit que passer dans [son] esprit de ce jour-là,—le temps d'y déposer quelque semonce imperceptible qui se développa un peu plus tard, dans un travail de plusieurs années.[3]

Speaking quite generally, the full significance of the first stage of preparation is that the poet can discover and quite

---

[1] *P.V.V.*, p. 290. Cf. a note in *Cahiers, tome sixième*, p. 752, written in 1917: "Avant la J P je me sentais me faisant l'instrument. Et nunc, je me sens l'instrument."

[2] *Fragments des mémoires d'un poème, Var. V*, p. 100.   [3] *Ibid.*, pp. 100, 101.

consciously act upon a number of principles which will eventually have an important bearing on poetic production. Though the discovery and the consequent action can be fairly conscious, their aim is to bring about an eventual integrated state of the poet where the benefits will arise spontaneously. It is probable that every good poet goes through something similar to this stage of preparation, though he will not usually bring to bear the same preoccupations, the same intent awareness, nor will he usually aspire to the same degree of knowledge and self-knowledge, control and self-control as Valéry during this stage. He will not usually be so articulate. Once again, it is a question of Valéry's consciously taking to extreme lengths tendencies present in many poets before him. His simple remark is incontrovertible:

> Personne a-t-il jamais songé à remontrer au musicien que les longues années qu'il consume à étudier l'harmonie et l'orchestre exténuent son démon particulier? Pourquoi suspendre le poète à la faveur de l'instant même?[1]

STAGE II. ILLUMINATION

It has been seen that the "poetic state" is not confined to the composer of poems, though it is conceived as a *sine qua non* of poetic composition; it can be regarded as a state lasting for days or months or even, with interruptions and with varying intensities, for years in a person actually composing poetry. The "poetic state" and illumination can be considered as one stage in creation, the latter being an integral consequence of the former, and indeed the most important form it can take. In this section, we shall examine Valéry's views on what this stage is, how and why it comes, the degree of control, if any, which the poet can exercise over it, and, finally, its relationship with "intimation" or "attente."

The "poetic state" has those characteristics commonly attributed to the state of poetic inspiration; and this is largely

[1] *Ibid.*, p. 104.

true of its manifestation in the poet, illumination. It is involuntary, it can come suddenly and go just as suddenly. Thus Valéry explains:

> Je n'ai jamais fait de vers que dans des périodes de ma vie qui sont très espacés l'un de l'autre; dans l'intervalle, le vers ne me dit rien, je ne m'en occupe presque pas, mais tout à coup, il se produit je ne sais quelles circonstances, mettons astronomiques, que je me trouve dans une phase où les mots me chantent.[1]

It is characterized by its intensity and by a singular contentment communicated to the poet.[2]

Illumination is the point of departure for the composition of a poem. Valéry explained how he experienced two forms of illumination, verbal and rhythmic. The former came to him as a line of verse, a "fragment," a "membre de phrase,"[3] a "combinaison définie,"[4] or "groupement remarquable de termes qui nous offrent tout à coup un heureux composé."[5] The other form occurred when a particular poem

> a commencé en [lui] par la simple indication d'un rythme qui s'est peu à peu donné un sens.[6]

In fact, by his own confession, most of his poems started with a rhythmical inspiration.[7] Yet

> chaque œuvre eût pu être produite par plusieurs voies. Rien ne nous montre dans un examen objectif si tel poème est né d'un certain hémistiche donné, d'une rime, ou d'un projet abstraitement formulé.[8]

—or, he might have added, from a rhythm. He is aware that

---

[1] *Souvenirs poétiques*, p. 32.
[2] Cf. *Fragments des mémoires d'un poème*, Var. V, p. 113.
[3] *La Création artistique*, Vues, p. 307.
[4] *Fragments des mémoires d'un poème*, Var. V, p. 113.   [5] *Ibid.*
[6] *Ibid.*, p. 92.   [7] Lefèvre, *Entretiens avec Paul Valéry*, p. 62.
[8] *La Création artistique*, Vues, p. 302.

different poets have different methods. It is to be noted, however, that he seems to have experienced personally only the two methods mentioned; he has never admitted that a "projet abstraitement formulé" gave a *start* to one of his own poems. When he mentions the possibility of such a project constituting the start of a poetic composition, he immediately says that such a method seems to be characteristic of big, long works, epics, dramatic poems, tragedies, comedies, and that

> les poèmes de ce genre sont ceux où l'on discerne le moins bien le caractère spécifique de la poésie, lequel consiste dans une improbable correspondance réciproque entre une forme sensible et une valeur significative.[1]

We remember his dictum:

> Si tu veux faire des vers et que tu commences par des pensées, tu commences par de la prose.[2]

The fact is that when he gives from his own experience instances of verbal illuminations, they impose themselves as much by their form as by their meaning. In short, his illuminations seem to be either rhythmical or a combination of *fond* and *forme*.

Valéry affirmed that what we here understand by verbal and rhythmical illuminations were different and distinct:

> J'ai trouvé une fois un simple rythme, et une autre fois, dans un autre cas, un distique qui représentait un membre de phrase et qui nécessitait logiquement un complément qui l'expliquait, et alors, cet élément complet, puisqu'il contenait à la fois le mot et le rythme et même la rime, a pu suggérer ce qui était au-dessus et au-dessous. Pour moi, ce sont deux cas très nets.[3]

It is not certain that the two illuminations are so distinguishable, even in the light of Valéry's own experience. The uncertainty can perhaps be resolved if we examine Valéry's own

---

[1] *Ibid.*   [2] *Calepin d'un poète, Poésies*, p. 186.
[3] *La Création artistique, Vues*, pp. 307, 308.

analysis of one of his rhythmical illuminations. There are three clear stages from the rhythm to the first line of poetry formed. In the first place, he is obsessed by a certain rhythm

> qui se fit tout à coup très sensible à [son] esprit, après un temps pendant lequel [il n'avait] qu'une demi-conscience de cette activité *latérale*. Ce rythme s'imposait à [lui], avec une sorte d'exigence.[1]

The second stage is explained thus:

> Il [lui] semblait qu'il [le rythme] voulût prendre un corps, arriver à la perfection de l'être. Mais il ne pouvait devenir plus net à [sa] conscience qu'en empruntant en quelque sorte des éléments *dicibles*, des syllabes, des mots, et ces syllabes et ces mots étaient sans doute, à ce point de la formation, déterminés par leur valeur et leurs attractions musicales. C'était là un état d'ébauche, un état enfantin, dans lequel la forme et la matière se distinguent peu l'une de l'autre, la forme rythmique constituant à ce moment l'unique condition d'admission, ou d'émission.[2]

We can compare this account with the two similar accounts of rhythmical illumination in *Fragments des mémoires d'un poème* [3] and *Poésie et pensée abstraite*.[4] They illustrate the point made in our introduction, namely, that the "poetic state," and even, in this case, a particular illumination resulting from it, is conceived as the essential experience which all the arts,—poetry, music, painting and architecture—derive from and seek to recreate in their various ways. The rhythmical illumination described here, if it had occurred in a person with musical gifts and training, might have sought expression through pure musical sounds rather than through words. It is to be remarked that consciousness gradually grows stronger in the poet as the third stage approaches (Valéry mentions the "demi-conscience" of the initial stage). The poet is beginning, however slightly, to exercise a degree of control over his illumination, as more of

---

[1] *Ibid.*, p. 300.   [2] *Ibid.*   [3] In *Var. V.*   [4] *Ibid.*

his mind and emotions become involved. Thus, for the third stage, he notes:

> Il arrive ensuite que, par une sorte d'éveil de la conscience ou d'extension assez brusque de son domaine—extension qualitative, bien entendu, accroissement du nombre des exigences indépendantes,—il se produit une substitution des syllabes et des mots provisoirement appelés, et qu'un certain *vers* initial se trouva non seulement tout fait, mais m'apparut comme impossible à modifier, comme l'effet d'une nécessité. Mais ce vers à son tour exigeait une suite musicale et logique. Le doigt était dans l'engrenage.[1]

Immediately after this description, he gives an instance of a verbal illumination:

> Dans un autre cas, un *vers* s'est présenté à moi, visiblement engendré par sa sonorité, par son timbre.

And he recounts, as above, the process of proliferation which followed this line of poetry. One is struck by the fact that this verbal illumination seems almost to overlap the third stage of the rhythmical illumination previously described. It could be that he either forgot afterwards, or for some reason was not at the time of illumination conscious of, the existence of two earlier stages which would be approximately those described for the rhythmical illumination. This interpretation is no doubt impertinent in that if anyone was conscious of the working of his own mind, it was Valéry. Nevertheless, it does seem permissible to consider the two illuminations as examples of "forme sensible" even if they are, so to speak, different sub-divisions of it. It would perhaps be safest and wisest to conclude that Valéry realized that many poets start a poem from a "projet abstraitement formulé;" he never did because such a beginning to a poem indicates a conception of poetry and poetic composition quite alien to him. Illumination for him as the start to a poem was never of sense alone,

---

[1] *La Création artistique, Vues*, p. 301.

but either exclusively (if only for a very short time) of form or of a composite nature, embracing sense and form. When it is exclusively formal illumination, then it is rhythmical; when it is composite the formal aspect is revealed by the sound or musical aspect which imposes itself simultaneously on the poet. Needless to say, in the light of his explanations, it is only a matter of seconds or minutes before there is bound to be an interaction of sound and sense.

★

When Valéry tries to discover why the "poetic state" and illumination come, and what degree of control the poet can exercise over them, he is more tentative and has little to tell us. The following sentences, for instance, are largely a restatement of the definition already given of the "poetic state" in so far as it occasions poetic composition:

> J'ai donc observé en moi-même tels états que je puis bien appeler *Poétiques*, puisque quelques-uns d'entre eux se sont finalement achevés en poèmes. Ils se sont produits sans cause apparente, à partir d'un accident quelconque; ils se sont développés selon leur nature, et par là, je me suis trouvé écarté pendant quelque temps de mon régime mental le plus fréquent. Puis, je suis revenu à ce régime d'échanges ordinaires entre ma vie et mes pensées, mon cycle étant achevé. Mais il était arrivé qu'*un poème avait été fait*, et que le cycle, dans son accomplissement, laissait quelque chose après soi.[1]

One explanation is offered by Valéry when he observes that

> tandis qu' [il se] livrait à diverses recherches qui n'avaient rien de littéraire, toutefois le démon ou le sens de l'art veillait au fond de [son] esprit.[2]

This tentative notion leads him, when attempting to explain the arrival of the "poetic state," to this conjecture:

---

[1] *Poésie et pensée abstraite, Var. V*, p. 135.
[2] *La Création artistique, Vues*, p. 286.

Peut-être y a-t-il en nous une mémoire périodique et lente, plus profonde que la mémoire des impressions et des objets, une mémoire ou une résonance de nous-mêmes à longue échéance, qui nous rapporte, et vient nous rendre à l'improviste nos tendances, nos puissances, et même nos espoirs très anciens?[1]

The notion of a periodic memory can be linked with another statement which could be considered as an adumbration of the 'buried stream' theory:[2]

Or, d'assez graves inquiétudes étaient venues traverser cette vie d'apparence stationnaire, qui n'absorbait ni n'émettait rien [Valéry is referring to his life in 1913]; d'autre part, une certaine lassitude de sa longue persévérance dans des voies assez abstraites se prononçant; et enfin, *ce qu'on-ne-peut-savoir* (comme l'âge ou tel point critique de l'organisme) agissant, il se fit ce qu'il fallait pour que la poésie pût reprendre quelque puissance en moi, si l'occasion s'en présentait.[3]

The kind reader might interpret the phrase "il se fit ce qu'il fallait" as revealing Valéry's desire not to bore with details which he could give if he wished; but it is possible to see disingenuousness or ignorance in it. The "occasion," the "accident quelconque" was the timely intervention of Gide and Gallimard when they asked him to consider for publication the collection they had made of his early verse. His account of how he thus returned to poetic creation is well known—how at first he glanced grudgingly over this collection, gradually began to toy with words and slowly warmed to the task as the "poetic state" and later, illumination, came to him. The 'buried stream' rises to the surface again, but, since Valéry is no

---

[1] *Le Prince et la Jeune Parque, Var. V*, p. 119.
[2] F. Scarfe refuses, perhaps too readily, to explore this theory with regard to Valéry. (*The Art of Paul Valéry—A Study in Dramatic Monologue*, London, Heinemann, Glasgow University Publications XCVII, 1954, p. 29).
[3] *Fragments des mémoires d'un poème, Var. V*, p. 100.

longer the same man, it inevitably differs from the poetic stream of his youth. As he explains in *La Création artistique* and *Fragments des mémoires d'un poème*, despite the "poetic state" and illumination, he attempts to annex poetic composition to his "diverses recherches qui n'avaient rien de littéraire"[1] by seeking to be as conscious as possible during actual composition in order to find out what he can about his "fonctionnement d'ensemble."

He was tired of the abstractions which had occupied him for so long. His pride was involved in that it occurred to him that he ought to give some tangible proof of the efficacy of his "method." Thus he writes:

> Tandis que je m'abandonnais avec d'assez grandes jouissances à des réflexions de cette espèce, et que je trouvais dans la poésie un sujet de questions infinies, la même conscience de moi-même qui m'y engageait me représentait qu'une spéculation, sans quelque production d'œuvres ou d'actes qui la puissent vérifier est chose trop douce pour ne pas devenir, si profonde ou si ardue qu'on la poursuive en soi, une tentation prochaine de facilité sous des apparences abstraites.[2] Je m'apercevais que ce qui désormais m'intéressait dans cet art était la quantité d'esprit qu'il me semblait pouvoir développer, et qu'il excitait d'autant plus qu'on se faisait de lui une idée plus approfondie. Je ne voyais pas moins nettement que toute cette dépense d'analyse ne pouvait prendre un sens et une valeur que moyennant une pratique et une production qui s'y rapportât.[3]

It is not clear from his account just when this last idea occurred to him; it may have been more or less unconsciously one of the factors leading to the return of the "poetic state," but it seems to have played a conscious rôle only after the latter had

[1] See p. 122, note 2.

[2] Cf. *Cahiers, tome quatrième*, p. 643, where he observes that *his* works have yet to appear. The works of others are at least written—"ce qui n'est pas indifférent."

[3] *Fragments des mémoires d'un poème, Var. V*, p. 107.

returned in the way he describes, through the intervention of Gide and Gallimard.

Marcel Raymond favours the notion implicit in the 'buried stream' theory, and, in the light of Valéry's own statements, his view seems sound when he writes:

> Si la conscience, en sa fonction normale, fait le vide, la sensibilité, elle, 'a horreur du vide'. Ainsi donc, la mystique de la vie (ou 'de la sensation de vivre') ne peut s'instaurer qu'au défaut de l'ascèse de l'intellect, et grâce à un régime d'intermittences. Il y a nécessairement rupture, et passage du vide au plein, du refus à l'acceptation.[1]

—There is acceptance of "la mystique de la vie," and, at the same time, the lowering of the barriers against sensibility of which the "poetic state" and illumination essentially consist. Given the "accident" of Gide's and Gallimard's intervention, Valéry got the "poetic state" and illumination because he was ready for them and wanted them. He himself stresses at various times the rôle which relaxed consciousness plays in the coming of inspiration. One might say that relaxed consciousness is characteristic of a period of Valéry's life, starting in 1913 (and ending in 1922?) and also characteristic, in a more complete manner, of those moments during which illumination came to him during the period. Ribot, in his *Essai sur l'imagination créatrice*, hazards this generalization:

> L'inspiration n'est pas une cause, mais plutôt un effet—plus exactement un moment, une crise, un état aigu: c'est un *indice*. Elle marque ou bien la *fin* d'une élaboration inconsciente . . . , ou bien le *commencement* d'une élaboration consciente . . . (ceci se rencontre surtout dans les cas de créations suggérées par le hasard).[2]

Valéry's inspiration could be seen as belonging to both types. There was a conscious effort for about twenty years with a non-poetic aim, which was at the same time an unconscious

---

[1] M. Raymond, *Sur les traces de Valéry*, in *P.V.V.*, p. 342.
[2] Th. Ribot, *Essai sur l'imagination créatrice*, Paris, Alcan, 1926, p. 49.

elaboration in relation to the poetic creation to come after 1913. Then, once he had returned to poetic creation, he practises, as we know, fairly conscious elaboration of the illumination afforded him.

Valéry's views on the second stage of creation are linked quite clearly with certain of his views on the "fonctionnement d'ensemble." Illumination has an obvious connection with the "moi instantané" which gives

> le choc initial qui constituera un commencement, et puis des valeurs de sensibilité.[1]

Illumination might be considered as a product of the "moi instantané," occurring further along the path which leads from the latter to the "moi complet," but still far removed from full 'awareness'. It is significant that, in one of his *cours de poétique*, he explains that it is just after the stage of the "moi instantané" that

> nous avons chance de trouver quelques notions, quelques voies nouvelles sur cette sorte de chemin des possibilités successives [i.e. the path from "moi instantané" to "moi complet"].[2]

The "moi instantané" and the illumination are essentially derived from sensibility. He affirms that

> la sensibilité à l'état pur est une mine de trouvailles et une mine de relations implicites, de combinaisons vierges.[3]

We are thus brought back to his general admission that the poet must benefit from 'intermittent' and 'primary intuitive inspiration' at the beginning of a given poem.

Valéry has a very limited knowledge of the second stage of creation and little control over it:

Pour l'artiste, l'état initial est indéfinissable. Le terme 'in-

---

[1] *Cours de poétique* of 4 March 1938.
[2] *Cours de poétique* of 12 March 1938.
[3] *Cours de poétique* of 18 February 1938.

définissable' a ici valeur positive. C'est un élément positif qui apparaît lorsque nous sommes en présence de certaines émotions. Est indéfinissable l'état qu'il n'est pas pour nous possible de retrouver par certains actes donnés. Des choses sont au delà de l'acte. Elles constituent la catégorie de l'indéfinissable.[1]

Moreover, however well he explains, on the one hand, the nature of the "poetic state," and, on the other hand, illumination and the work of composition by the poet, he gives no conclusive explanation why the "poetic state" gives the illumination it does to the poet. It is true that this is partly accounted for by the poet's preparation and his interest and training in language. But this explanation merely serves to raise another essential problem: what is a gift for language, how does one explain that nature which can, in the form of illumination, derive from the "poetic state" a profit for purposes of composition?

*

There is one last aspect of illumination to mention in this section—"intimation." The second stage of creation marks the beginning of the "état initial indéfinissable," [2] but it also gives to the poet a certain impetus for composition; a certain compulsion is on him which leads his thought to proliferate from what is given by the illumination, thenceforth composing within a certain not too restricted field of possibilities hinted at [3] by the illumination. Here is one good account among several that Valéry gives of this phenomenon:

Dans un autre cas, un *vers* s'est présenté à moi, visiblement engendré par sa sonorité, par son timbre. Le sens que suggérait cet élément inattendu de poème, l'image qu'il évoquait, sa figure syntaxique (une apposition), agissant

---

[1] *Cours de poétique* of 11 December 1937, in *Yggdrasill* of 25 January 1938.
[2] *Ibid.*
[3] Valéry used the words "imminence" and "imminent" to convey this idea.

comme agit un petit cristal dans une solution sursaturée, m'ont conduit comme par symétrie à *attendre*, et à construire selon cette attente, en deça et au delà de ce vers, un commencement qui préparât et justifiât son existence, et une suite qui lui donnât son plein effet. Ainsi, de ce seul vers, sont provenus de proche en proche tous les éléments d'un poème, le sujet, le ton, le type prosodique . . . etc.[1]

When, after explaining how a particular rhythmical illumination led to "un certain vers initial," he writes:

Mais ce vers à son tour exigeait une suite musicale et logique,[2]

the chances are that he was experiencing "intimation" here also. There are two ways of accounting for the progression from illumination to composition. On the one hand, we assume that he wants to compose a poem even before he experiences the "poetic state." He is then in the position of many poets; the desire helps to engender the "poetic state;" he becomes sensitized to that state and to certain sounds, and, after a given period of incubation, he obtains an illumination; once he has obtained it, he is willing and able to make use of it by the process of proliferation he describes, or by what appears to be a similar but rather more cerebral and calculating method such as is described in *Au sujet du Cimetière Marin*.[3] If on the other hand the "poetic state" descends on him at a moment when he is not particularly wanting to compose a poem, then it gives the illumination, verbal or rhythmical, which makes him willing and able to start composition. The illumination carries with it a certain impetus ("exigence"), a sort of stage, half intellect, half sensibility, as he sketches out, very approximately, the next line before or after, and even a rough idea of the whole poem. (All this adumbration, of course, will be eventually subject to great modification, as we shall see). Valéry either wants to compose a poem in any case, or illumination is an even more compulsive form of inspiration than might have

---

[1] *La Création artistique, Vues*, p. 301.   [2] *Ibid.*   [3] In *Var. III.*

been supposed. The second alternative is clearly his usual experience.

It follows that his frequently drawn distinction, in various formulae, between "sentir" and "rendre sensible," or more narrowly, between the "poetic state" experienced by a sizeable number of people and poetic composition, does not do full justice to the reality of the poetic process as he himself at other times reveals it. Valéry often seems to make even greater than it is the gulf which lies between feeling in a poetic way and actually composing a poem. It is no doubt true that, without the first stage of preparation, the "poetic state" would not lead to the composition of a good poem however strong the impetus or urge to compose communicated by illumination, but the fact remains that, given "intimation," illumination plays an even bigger part than Valéry sometimes leads his readers to suppose.

STAGE III. COMPOSITION: THE POET AT WORK

The third stage comprehends all that occurs from the latter part of 'primary intuitive inspiration,' that is, illumination, to the poem as read by the reader (Valéry would not have spoken of the *finished* poem). He gives no entirely fixed pattern for the kinds of inspiration or for the various steps which may be involved in this stage. The general lines, however, are clear enough.

He asserts quite dogmatically that

aussitôt que l'instinct ou l'impulsion poétique passe à l'action de produire, on peut observer que quelque chose d'analogue à un calcul se prononce ou se dessine dans l'esprit au travail, puisque quelque chose tend à se conserver et qu'une certaine forme se propage de proche en proche, condition même de l'unité d'un poème aussi bien que de tout calcul.[1]

The emphasis on calculation is derived from his early notion of

---

[1] *Le Cas Servien*, in *op. cit.* by P. Servien, pp. 87, 88.

the poem as "une machine poétique," as an "*effet* à produire." [1] The categorical nature of his views on this point is brought out by the words we have italicized in the following restatement:

> Cette première phase [i.e. the "poetic state" and illumination] appartient en somme à la psychologie générale. Les événements qui s'y produisent, quoique essentiels à la création dont ils accumulent la substance générale,—sous forme d'éléments émotifs, d'associations particulièrement heureuses ou puissantes—toutefois sont loin de suffire à la production de l'ouvrage organisé. Celle-ci implique un ordre tout différent d'activité mentale. L'auteur, *qu'il s'en doute ou non*, prend une attitude toute nouvelle. Il ne voyait d'abord qu'en soi-même; mais à peine songe-t-il à une œuvre, il entre dans un calcul d'effets extérieurs. C'est un problème d'accommodation qui se pose: il se préoccupe *sciemment ou inconsciemment* des sujets sur lesquels doit agir son ouvrage, il se fait une idée de ceux qu'il visa et il se représente, d'autre part, les moyens dont il peut disposer pour cette action. [2]

The entering into play of this element of calculation coincides with the fading of the illumination which gave a start to the poem and with the greater degree of consciousness which gradually comes to the poet. In one of his *cours de poétique*, Valéry explains the same point by referring to some of the terms we examined in our second chapter. He says that if a given stimulus is strong enough, there follows inevitably a period of reflection, when the mind normally tries to get back to that state of balance and "availability" which he calls the "cours naturel." But with the poet,

> la réflexion recherche le niveau, ou le point de plus grande liberté à l'égard des possibilités pour retrouver à ce point la voie . . . non la voie du plus prompt retour à ce cours naturel des choses qui nous délivrera de l'impression, mais puisque nous cherchons au contraire à nous instruire à partir

---

[1] *P.V.V.*, p. 60.   [2] *La Création artistique, Vues*, p. 297.

d'impressions, nous chercherons la voie de la plus grande
nécessité ... c'est-à-dire de l'attachement le plus rigoureux
à un développement qui, lui, satisfasse à des conditions à
priori.[1]

We note again that he either takes for granted the desire to
compose or else presumes that the illumination carries with it
an impetus or compulsion to do so.

The dogmatic emphasis on calculation is associated with
Valéry's constant thesis that illumination provides "valeurs de
sensibilité," that the "moi instantané n'est capable d'aucune
opération," [2] and that it is the intelligence which seizes, evaluates
and usually modifies what has been supplied by illumination.
It is moreover clear that Valéry, as a poet, consciously carries
to an extreme limit a tendency, calculation, which he believes
to exist in all poets at this stage of creation—though they may
not all realize this fact. He admits that, very often, the poet
passes from the second to the third stage quickly:

> Chez l'artiste, il arrive en effet—c'est le cas le plus favo-
> rable,—que le même mouvement interne de production lui
> donne à la fois et indistinctement l'impulsion, le but extérieur
> immédiat et les moyens ou les dispositifs techniques de
> l'action.[3]

This is not usually true of his own composition, though it is
all a matter of degree. The last quotation seems to describe
what we have called "exalted inspiration," or the inspired
improvisation which remains rather an ideal for Valéry,
perhaps most nearly approached during the composition of
some poems in *Charmes*. As we have seen, the question of how
speedily and effectively the poet passes from the second to the
third stage is linked with Valéry's usual desire to distinguish
perhaps too trenchantly between the "poetic state" which may
remain an inarticulate private enjoyment and the third stage,

---

[1] *Cours de poétique* of 12 March 1938.
[2] *Cours de poétique* of 18 February 1938.
[3] *Cours de poétique*, *Var. V*, p. 321.

when it is necessary for the poet to make a deliberate effort to compose.

It is "intimation" that bridges the gap between the two stages.[1] Valéry believes that there are two states for the poet, which correspond to what we have called illumination and "intimation" (coupled with effort):

> l'un où celui qui fait son métier d'écrivain est traversé d'une sorte d'éclair; car enfin, cette vie intellectuelle et non passive se compose de fragments; elle est, en quelque sorte, formée d'éléments très brefs, mais qu'on sent très riches, qui n'éclairent pas tout l'esprit, qui lui indiquent, au contraire, qu'il y a des formes tout à fait neuves dont il est sûr qu'il les possédera par un certain travail. Ce que j'ai observé quelquefois, c'est l'arrivée d'une sensation de l'esprit, d'une lueur, non pas une lueur éclairante, mais fulgurante. Elle avertit, elle désigne beaucoup plus qu'elle n'éclaire, et en somme, elle est elle-même une énigme qui porte avec elle l'assurance qu'elle peut être différée. On dit: 'Je vois, et puis demain je verrai ensuite'. Un fait se produit, une sensibilisation spéciale; bientôt on ira dans la chambre noire et l'on verra apparaître l'image.[2]

Elsewhere, speaking of illumination, he writes:

> Il [l'instant . . . précieux] excite un contentement incomparable et une tentation immédiate; il fait espérer que l'on trouvera *dans son voisinage* tout un trésor dont il est le signe et la preuve; et cet espoir engage parfois son homme dans un travail qui peut être sans bornes.[3]

"Intimation," or what Roger Callois has happily described as "une certaine exigence de croissance,"[4] is thus vital during

---

[1] Cf. *Cahiers, tome sixième*, p. 658: "L'attente est la sensation de l'état intermédiaire—L'inspiration est l'invasion au *moment* du besoin de l'idée dont on avait précisément besoin."

[2] *La Création artistique, Vues*, p. 304.

[3] *Fragments des mémoires d'un poème, Var. V*, p. 113.

[4] Roger Callois, *Les Impostures de la poésie*, Paris, Gallimard, 1945, p. 51.

the third stage of creation. The poet is able to adumbrate perhaps the whole poem, perhaps only a part of it, or only certain aspects of it. Given the fact that Valéry, like any poet, had general notions of what poetry should be, and especially what his own poetry should be, he was able to derive particular notions of what a given poem should be like from the "intimation" left behind by the illumination (see, for example, what he has to say about the poem's structure, verse-form, and subject in *Au sujet du Cimetière Marin*).[1] His statements about illumination and "intimation" show that his experiences are similar to those of many poets, for whom Sir Maurice Bowra can serve as spokesman:

> In this process, what begins by being unconscious becomes conscious; what is at the start an outburst of energy infused with a vague idea of an undifferentiated form becomes concrete and definite; what is outside the poet's control is gradually made to submit to his will and judgement. Such, or something like it, seems to be the usual experience of poets, and such primarily inspiration is.[2]

Sir Maurice stresses the point made by Valéry regarding the confidence which the poet feels, confidence given by "intimation" that he will be able, if only slowly and with effort, to find what he needs for the structure which will become a poem:

> While such a fit is on him, the poet has a sense of inexhaustible abundance and does not question that the visitation will give him all, and more than all, that he needs for his task.[3]

The confidence that, with "intimation," the poem can be got by effort is important in that it enables the poet to devote all his attention to the task of composition.

[1] In *Var. III*, pp. 63, 64.   [2] C. M. Bowra, *op. cit.*, p. 5.
[3] *Ibid.* Valéry would not perhaps have liked the vocabulary—"fit", "inexhaustible"—and would not have concurred unconditionally with the notion of facility implied, but the substance of Bowra's statement is implicit in Valéry's ideas on the point involved.

The illumination thus gives a pattern,[1] a field or framework in which the poet can work, relying on "intimation" to clothe this framework, so that a poem is slowly formed. Valéry emphasizes that the poet has to set himself to compose within this framework by a combination of conscious effort and waiting for the psychic mechanism set up to give results.[2] Thus he writes:

> Le poète en fonction est une *attente*. Il est une modification dans un homme,—qui le fait sensible à certains *termes* de son propre développement: ceux qui récompensent cette attente pour être conformes à la convention. Il restitue ce qu'il désirait.[3]

In the light of these considerations, he is led to suggest that creative discovery, where a limited degree of control is exercised as we have seen, is only a less conscious and less certain form of choice:

> J'estime que le *choix* est proche parent de l'*invention*, et que la différence se réduit peut-être à celle du simple et du complexe. Il y a choix, il n'y que choix quand l'ensemble des possibilités est un ensemble d'objets simples ou éléments définis par une seule qualité, que l'on peut rapporter à une

---

[1] Robin Skelton notes that many poets have had a similar experience: "Whether or not the poet is in a state of deep trance, we may say with some certainty that he or she has some intuition of the shape of the poem that is to come, and that the 'spirit' of Miss Raine, the 'vague notion of the poem' of Housman, the 'nucleus' of Robert Graves, the 'rhythm' of Valéry, and the musical mood of Schiller are different interpretations of the same experience; and that it is not entirely unjust to say that this intuition which precedes the arrival of the poem has as its main element the seldom fully conscious perception of a pattern, whether musical or visual, logical or sensual" (*The Poetic Pattern*, London, Routledge and Kegan Paul, 1956, p. 17).

[2] Cf. *Cahiers, tome quatrième*, p. 337: "J'ai fait de l'attention autour de telle question—je n'arrive pas—mais j'ai mis en train un mouvement qui m'échappe et pendant mon sommeil—ce mouvement commencé continue indépendamment. Au réveil je trouve la solution."

[3] *Calepin d'un poète, Poésies*, p. 183.

gamme, comme les couleurs. Dans ce cas, nous cherchons à nous placer dans un état tel que notre décision soit automatique; nous cherchons à nous trouver une sorte de *tropisme*. Mais si les objets sont très complexes, il se fera un effort en nous pour construire l'état parfois inaccessible qui devrait aboutir à nous faire émettre, à tirer de nous une décision aussi immédiate que la précédente. Cet effort est semiconscient, et il est invention.[1]

When the objects are of the greatest complexity, people speak of *inspiration*, that is to say, of a choice which is not even semiconscious; the steps which led to it cannot be retraced. The whole problem, in the complex matter of poetry, lies in the degree of control, and, to a lesser extent, of consciousness, obtained by the poet. The mature Valéry seems often to be content with empirical control without necessarily having the consciousness which he would have deemed essential in his youth. He knows that the poet is far from having complete control of invention or association. One important aspect of his notion of "intimation" is precisely the fact that it implies only a limited control, with uncertainty as to the results:

> En effet, nous ne pouvons agir directement que sur la liberté du système de notre esprit. Nous abaissons le degré de cette liberté, mais quant au reste, je veux dire quant aux modifications et aux substitutions que cette contrainte laisse possibles, nous attendons simplement que ce que nous désirons se produise, car nous ne pouvons que l'attendre. Nous n'avons aucun moyen d'atteindre exactement en nous ce que nous souhaitons en obtenir.[2]

---

[1] *La Création artistique, Vues*, p. 309.
[2] *Cours de poétique, Var. V*, p. 315. Cf. *Cahiers, tome troisième*, p. 459: "Nous n'avons pas d'action directe sur nos pensées. Nous faisons cuire, nous remuons—mais les transformations obtenues ne sont pas directement issues de nos actes. Nous mettons en présence—grossièrement; nous favorisons, amorçons nous comptons sur des *affinités* et sur des liens souterrains nous essayons de provoquer quelque chose plus profonde plus puissante, plus— savante! que nous."

"Abaisser le degré de la liberté du système de [son] esprit" —that is all he can do. But what happens in his mind when he is waiting for the solution he wants? We know so little, Valéry answers. No one would deny that our real knowledge is very limited, but, since he does offer suggestions, he could have gone on to say that it is because the ideas (to some extent controlled) set going certain feelings (barely controlled) that the poetic material he desires eventually emerges.[1] It has been claimed that

the ideas connected with a favourite study appear to acquire a certain tone which binds them together as an interest, so that when the thinker gets into a mood associated with this subject all relevant ideas in any way connected with it tend to come together or at any rate to become available. On the other hand the mood tends to act as a sieve which prevents the entry of irrelevant ideas, allowing only those which are relevant to enter ... Many ideas outside the subject become associated with it by a kind of interest association and acquire a similar tone ... The variety of interests tends to increase the richness of these extra ideas—'fringe-ideas'— associated with the subject and thus to increase the possibilities of new and original combinations of thought.[2]

Such considerations lead us to conclude that, during composition, and particularly during the states of "intimation," Valéry is having recourse to association by feeling, mood, by what constitutes his deepest self[3] (though he will still examine

---

[1] But Valéry asserts categorically in *Cahiers, tome cinquième*, p. 15: "Le sentiment ou ce qu'on appelle de ce nom n'est pour rien dans l'invention, dans la trouvaille réelle du musicien et du poète.

"Les trouvailles véritables,—résultent d'une sorte de cristallisation brusque ou semi brusque. C'est un *rangement sui generis* issu du *hasard*—le hasard lui-même ou nombre de circonstances peut comprendre le sentiment, émotion mais à titre d'élément."

[2] Rosamond E. M. Harding, *An Anatomy of Inspiration*, Cambridge, W. Heffer & Sons Ltd., 1948, p. 6.

[3] Valéry affirmed that "le plaisir littéraire n'est pas d'exprimer sa pensée tant que de trouver ce qu'on n'attendait pas de soi" (*Cahiers, tome sixième*, p. 783).

and evaluate, reject, accept or modify poetic material which emerges in the light of a general view of the poem composed so far). It is during such recourse to deep feeling that he obtains his "objective correlatives," [1] his "self-confirming perceptions," [2] something not very different from what Coleridge called

a symbolic language for something within [him] that forever and already exists.[3]

One could instance Valéry's pomegranates, the sun, the sky and the sea in Le Cimetière Marin.[4] Despite his reference to sensibility as a "mine de trouvailles . . . de combinaisons vierges,"[5] he is usually unwilling to examine the full implications of some of his views which have led us to stress the fundamental importance of feeling and mood in composition. Though he was, in fact, a man of powerful feeling, he always distrusted it and fought against it.[6]

It was claimed by Coleridge that

association depends in a much greater degree on the recurrence of resembling states of feeling than on trains of ideas.[7]

J. E. Downey writes of "affective spread or transfer" and explains how, in her view, feelings can be for a time "detached"

[1] The expression is T. S. Eliot's.
[2] The phrase is used by Sir Kenneth Clark in Moments of Vision, (The Romanes Lecture), Oxford, Clarendon Press, 1954, p. 19.
[3] Quoted by Sir Kenneth Clark, ibid., p. 16.
[4] See his sonnet Les Grenades, in Charmes, and L. J. Austin, La Genèse du CIMETIÈRE MARIN, Cahiers de l'Association internationale des Etudes françaises, July 1953, for his careful examination of the poem in the light of Valéry's admissions in Inspirations méditerranéennes, Var. III.
[5] Cours de poétique of 18 February 1938.
[6] Cf. Cahiers, tome huitième, p. 654: "au fond, je suis en proie au mépris de mes sentiments, qui sont malheureusement très vifs et très cruels en moi. Mon esprit en a souffert infiniment, et jamais cependant ne s'y est livré sans honte et sans colère."
[7] Quoted by I. A. Richards in Coleridge on Imagination, London, Routledge and Kegan Paul Ltd., 1950, p. 19.

free floating affects ready to attach themselves to stray percepts or ideas.[1]

She maintains that

aesthetic experience is largely concerned with the projection of affective reactions into an external world; it is an objectification of emotions; the creation of a universe of mood values ... Self is the very core of such creation since it is in process of externalizing itself.[2]

One might therefore claim that during poetic composition Valéry is doing more deliberately and with greater, though still very limited, consciousness what all poets do, bringing to the surface and objectifying in language his deepest feeling, associations of images and sounds personal to him. These associations provide what Robin Skelton calls *the pattern*. The unity of the poem is provided as much by mood values as by the conscious effort of the poet who works on their products. We can link this tapping of the deepest self with our notion of inspiration as an 'inspiring principle'—'personal inspiration' —and with the mature Valéry's conception of it.

The illumination and resulting "intimation" which the poet has may lead to further illuminations and "intimations." Valéry, much more than perhaps any other poet, emphasizes how the product (verbal or rhythmical) of any illumination or "intimation" needs to be examined in the dark room, so to speak:

ici, pas d'enthousiasme, car vous gâcheriez votre plaque, il faut employer vos réactifs, il faut travailler comme l'employé de vous-même, votre contre-maître. Le patron vous a fourni l'étincelle; c'est à vous d'en tirer quelque chose.[3]

The poet must ask himself whether the product is good, whether it is usable in the part of the poem so far composed, now that the euphoria noted as attendant on illumination has

---

[1] J. E. Downey, *op. cit.*, p. 130.   [2] *Ibid.*, pp. 177, 178.
[3] *La Création artistique, Vues*, pp. 304, 305.

faded away. Like Poincaré in his *Science et méthode*,[1] Valéry observes that this verification (seen by Graham Wallas as the essential part of the stage which, in all creative thought, follows illumination) may bring big disappointments: the product may have no intrinsic merit, it may have intrinsic merit but not 'fit' into the poem, despite conscious attempts to modify it so that it does:

> Ce qui est très curieux, c'est la déception qui peut s'ensuivre. Il y a des lueurs illusoires; en revoyant le résultat obtenu, le contremaître s'aperçoit que ce n'était pas fécond, c'eût été très bien si cela avait été vrai.[2]

One of Valéry's favourite themes was that of the poet's need for "refusals." A solution may be accepted for the time being and changed or removed later if a better one is forthcoming or if the future development of the poem changes the poet's earlier intention.

"Intimation" is clearly connected with what Graham Wallas calls "fringe-consciousness."[3] The poet senses that there is potential poetic material (a solution to a problem, an idea, a rhythm, a rhyme, a new development in the poem) just 'round the corner', psychologically speaking, which he will

---

[1] Cf. the following lines from Poincaré's *L'Invention mathématique*, in *Science et Méthode*, Paris, Flammarion, 1947, p. 62, where the parallel with Valéry's ideas is obvious: "il n'arrive jamais que le travail inconscient nous fournisse *tout fait* le résultat d'un calcul un peu long, où l'on n'a qu'à appliquer des règles fixes... Tout ce qu'on peut espérer de ces inspirations, qui sont les fruits du travail inconscient, ce sont des points de départ pour de semblables calculs; quant aux calculs eux-mêmes, il faut les faire dans la second période de travail conscient, celle qui suit l'inspiration; celle où l'on vérifie les résultats de cette inspiration et où l'on en tire les conséquences. Les règles de ces calculs sont strictes et compliquées; elles exigent la discipline, l'attention, la volonté, et par suite, la conscience. Dans le moi subliminal règne, au contraire, ce que j'appellerais la liberté, si l'on pouvait donner ce nom à la simple absence de discipline et au désordre né du hasard. Seulement, ce désordre même permet des accouplements inattendus."

[2] *La Création artistique, Vues*, p. 305.

[3] G. Wallas, *op. cit.*, p. 52. Wallas takes the word "fringe" from William James.

probably be able to seize if he waits a while until this fringe-consciousness becomes "focal," to use Wallas's term. The poet must bring to bear for this capture a certain will and effort. The fringe-consciousness has to be coaxed into fuller and clearer existence.[1] He must avoid letting it disappear, as it might easily if it is not coaxed and if he does not immediately jot down all suggestions which come into his full focal consciousness. Valéry's manuscripts reveal this jotting down of suggestions and provisionally accepted findings more abundantly than is the case with many poets. Rudolf Arnheim notes this aspect of poets' manuscripts with a useful image:

> The indefiniteness of words ... suggests that the literary recording of an experience resembles, in its first stages, the trapping of an insect with a large net. The little animal is being confined to a limited area but not yet pinned to a specific spot. The work sheets show how the poet closes in gradually on the adequate formulation.[2]

Auden was making much the same point when he wrote:

> How can I know what I think till I see what I say? A poet writes 'The chestnut's comfortable root' and then changes this to 'The chestnut's customary root'. In this alteration there is no question of replacing one emotion by another,[3]

[1] Thus, in *Cahiers, tome sixième*, p. 664, Valéry describes what is really a combination of "intimation," will and "improvisation de degré supérieur:" "Le monde de l'inspiration (qu'elle soit poétique ou scientifique) n'est autre d'ailleurs que celui—(ou le système vivant)—dans lequel est possible l'équivalence parfaite (à la limite) du désir et de ce qui la satisfait.
"Le système où ceci est possible est le système spirituel.
"Et dans ce monde-là, on peut supposer que le désir lui-même est créé par une première conscience de l'existence cachée ou *diffuse* de l'objet désirable, que nous ne cherchons jamais, *non sans l'avoir trouvé*, mais du moins sans le posséder en quelque manière."

[2] Rudolf Arnheim in *Poets at Work*, New York, Harcourt, Brace and Co., p. 147. In *Cahiers, tome sixième*, p. 66, Valéry says much the same thing with a different image: "Il s'agit de mettre une balle au centre de la cible. On tire n coups. Aprés quoi le coup n + 1 donne le but."

[3] In Valéry's case there often is. A new emotion may be the origin of a more acceptable poetic product.

or of strengthening an emotion, but of discovering what the emotion is. The emotion is unchanged, but waiting to be identified like a telephone number one cannot remember. '8357. No, that's not it. 8557, 8457, no, it's on the tip of my tongue, wait a moment, I've got it, 8657. That's it'.[1]

To capture what the poet, through "intimation," senses is there to be captured,—this requires, we have said, an effort of will. But, often, the effort must not be too strong or the capture will never be made:

> Nous devons donc passionnément attendre, . . . et vouloir, vouloir . . . Et même, ne pas excessivement vouloir.[2]

During composition, the poet has to know how to pass from active seeking to mere passive waiting and even to temporary forgetting.[3] The phenomenon is well known to most people when memory is involved, rather than invention, and is well described by Roger Callois:

> Chaque effort qu'on tente pour l'appréhender [i.e. un

---

[1] W. H. Auden, *Poets at Work*, op. cit., p. 174.

[2] *Au sujet d'Adonis*, Var. II, p. 78.

[3] Cf. *Cahiers, tome deuxième*, p. 237: "Un vertige commun est de prendre ce qui est confus et vague pour quelque chose qui pourrait être clair si. . Cependant c'est un procédé général et il est indispensable à l'invention comme moteur. Celui qui précise d'avance et ne peut voir que distinctement invente peu—mais celui qui ne précise jamais n'invente pas et pense au hasard. C'est donc une éducation ou don spécial qu'il faut et qui consiste dans l'emploi gradué de la précision, dans une intervention exquise chez un esprit.

"Il importe de laisser agir l'esprit sur un point donné avec sa suite naturelle, ne rien perdre de vue et cueillir mais sachant quel lien." In the same *cahier*, p. 278, Valéry affirms that "l'inconscience c'est le jeu même de la connaissance, son fonctionnement *incessant* et son entraînement. La conscience est une tentative pour juger ce jeu—le diriger et l'appliquer. Ces 2 choses ne s'opposent pas. La conscience n'a aucun pouvoir de production—mais de retard, de direction, de limitation, etc. et puis de *vision* plus ou moins nette. Or cette tentative fait partie elle aussi de la production.

"C'est une gymnastique encore inconnue que celle du balancement adroit de ces 2 propriétés. Il est clair qu'il faut savoir laisser produire—et savoir arrêter ou exciter à temps."

souvenir rebelle] fait plus clairement apercevoir que c'est l'effort même qui met en fuite l'objet de la quête. Il faut attendre de ne plus y penser. Alors se présente à l'esprit vide ou occupé d'un autre soin ce que sa fièvre ne réussit pas à saisir, quand il était plein de celui-là.[1]

But this is not the whole truth of the matter. Valéry believes that, even though the capture is often made in the manner described by Callois, the efforts which preceded the relaxation of effort were essential to set going a certain psychic process which is then, from the point of view of *rendement poétique*, beyond the poet's control.[2] His point is admirably made by André Spire:

Cette trouvaille est préparée par cette longue période de tension pendant laquelle le poète tâtonne, travaille par touches, approches successives, comme le peintre qui confronte ses couleurs, le mécanicien qui ajuste une pièce.[3]

To confirm this truth, we have only to examine some of the manuscripts of Valéry's poems. The various stages which resulted in the "Midi le juste" of *Le Cimetière Marin* are as good an instance as any.[4]

Frequent reliance on "intimation", which has an obvious, though limited, connection with conscious effort and planning, does not exclude recourse to chance, disorder and surprise— referred to in such sentences as:

---

[1] Callois, *op. cit.*, p. 58.

[2] Cf. *Cahiers, tome sixième*, p. 66: "Il s'agit de mettre une balle au centre de la cible. On tire n coups. Après quoi le coup $n+1$ donne le but. Entre n et $n+1$ quelque chose s'est produit. Quoi?

"Les coups préparatoires ont accru l'énergie disponible et assigné aussi les seules fonctions qui doivent enfin agir et *qui s'ignoraient au début*. On ne sait pas d'abord—et on ne distingue d'ailleurs jamais, quelles sont les fonctions qui agissent utilement enfin." Cf. also, in the same *cahier*, p. 651: "Trouver un vers, une mélodie, c'est entendre—attendre—Et alors,—on *reçoit toujours* —mais on reçoit ce que l'attente a formé—et on reçoit ce qu'on a *voulu* si l'attente formée est précisément conforme à ce qu'on a *conceptuellement voulu*."

[3] A. Spire, *op. cit.*, p. 58.

[4] See L. J. Austin, *op. cit.* (Grenoble, Roissard, 1954).

L'esprit fait des surprises à l'organisme; l'organisme en fait à l'esprit.[1]

Valéry, we have seen, knew how to benefit from what Roger Callois has called "une sorte très particulière de distraction féconde de l'esprit." [2] Walking seems to have been a favourite way in which he was able to profit from such a distraction.[3] During actual composition, he is always ready to use the material which arrives in a form not anticipated:

> C'est l'imprévu, le discontinu, la forme du réel et d'être à laquelle on n'avait jamais pensé,—qui font le charme et la force de l'observation et des expériences.
> On croyait contempler ou pressentir les solutions possibles et il y en a une autre ...[4]

More than this, since he knows by experience that such surprise solutions nearly always come during composition, he counts on them and is not averse to profiting from the subconscious, when the mind and body have had time to assimilate the data of a particular problem and eventually produce a *trouvaille*:

> Je ne sais ce que je ferai; et pourtant, mon esprit croit se connaître; et je bâtis sur cette connaissance, je compte sur elle, que j'appelle *Moi*. Mais *je me ferai une surprise*; si j'en doutais, je ne serais rien. Je sais que je m'étonnerai de telle pensée qui me viendra tout à l'heure,—et pourtant je me

---

[1] *M.P.*, p. 175.   [2] Callois, *op. cit.*, p. 51.
[3] See *Poésie et pensée abstraite, Var. V*, p. 139.
[4] *Analecta, T.Q. II*, p. 269. Cf. *Cahiers, tome quatrième*, p. 399: "Profiter de l'accident heureux—L'écrivain véritable abandonne son idée au profit d'une autre qui lui apparaît en cherchant les mots de la voulue, par les mots mêmes. Il se trouve devenu plus puissant, même plus profond par ce jeu de mots imprévu—mais dont il voit instantanément la valeur (= ce qu'un lecteur en tirera): c'est son mérite. Et il passe pour profond et créateur—n'ayant été que critique et chasseur foudroyant." The last words are a typical exaggeration. The poet's ability to produce is as important as his ability to capture and criticize.

demande cette surprise, je bâtis et je compte sur elle, comme je compte sur ma certitude. J'ai l'espoir de quelque imprévu que je désigne, j'ai besoin de mon connu et de mon inconnu.[1]

The word "intimation" can be susceptible of an extremely wide application. It can cover the state of the poet as he broods over the solution of a small, local problem in his poem; on the other hand, all the *lueurs* or illuminations of the third stage can be seen as the fruit of a long-term "intimation" based on the first stage and the whole life of the poet. Valéry's conception of "intimation" is linked with some of his other views on the "fonctionnement d'ensemble." We examined in our second chapter what he calls our "états d'attente," when

nous sommes accommodés, sans nous en douter, à des phénomènes qui peuvent se produire, et pas à d'autres.[2]

He envisages the poet as becoming conscious of the rôle which such states play, and learning to control as much as possible the "montage intérieur" [3] which they essentially are. The poet must know how to abandon himself to them at certain times, although he will always examine later any poetic material resulting from them. "Intimation" is linked particularly with Valéry's notion that sensibility abhors a vacuum.[4] If there is enough silence and relative freedom from external stimuli,

il y a changement qui consiste dans une production inévitable, incoercible d'effets psychiques et affectifs.[5]

Nondescript "effets psychiques et affectifs" are often of little use for purposes of poetic composition (though Valéry would presumably interpolate here that sometimes, and particularly if, illumination and "intimation" having faded, the poet has reached a state of impotence, they might provide a new and

[1] *Au sujet d'Adonis, Var. II*, pp. 82, 83.
[2] *Cours de poétique* of 18 February 1938.   [3] *P.V.V.*, p. 104.
[4] See *Léonard et les philosophes, Vinci*, p. 131, and also the *cours de poétique* of 17 December 1937, in *Yggdrasill* of 25 January 1938.
[5] *Cours de poétique* of 8 January 1938.

eventually profitable point of departure). Valéry therefore sets himself a difficult goal:

> Le zéro et la tension ne peuvent coexister. *Le silence et l'attention sont incompatibles.* Il faut que le courant soit fermé. Créer donc l'espèce de silence à laquelle répond le beau. Ou le vers pur, ou l'idée lumineuse . . .[1]

This formulation leads us back to the theme of preparation.

In a *cours de poétique* of 1938, he asks himself why a particular idea or word which occurs to him at a given moment solves or helps to solve some difficulty, in poetic composition or elsewhere. When he replies that it is all perhaps a simple question of "excitability" and time, we are scarcely enlightened. He suggests that

> telle zone a été atteinte au bout d'un temps assez court, pour qu'une première excitation n'ait pas eu le temps . . . de disparaître, de s'évanouir et puis de rejoindre deux choses qui seraient restées séparées.

He concludes that

> il arrive à chaque instant que nous serions pleins de génie, si nous pouvions rassembler une idée qui est venue à l'heure H, et une idée qui est venue à l'heure H plus 1.[2]

He is fascinated by this problem of adjustment and timing; he dreams of developing

> un instrument spécial, un appareil intérieur, une manière

---

[1] *Calepin d'un poète, Poésies*, p. 184.
[2] *Cours de poétique* of 7 January 1938. Cf. a letter to Pierre Louÿs in *Quinze lettres de Paul Valéry à Pierre Louÿs, lettre B:* "pour qui étudie le rêve, il y a des réveils qui sont des chances, des réveils qui par leur *époque* relative, par la phase du rêve *quelconque* qu'ils interrompent, par leur mode net de faire une coupe au bon moment, sont précieux à l'égal, par exemple, d'une 'inspiration', d'une 'bonne idée', etc. . . . Et peut-être, allons plus avant, peut-être, Seigneur, qu'une *bonne idée*, un éclair de génie, se ramènerait à un phénomène semblable (Avec un peu d'autre génie pour le démontrer)."

d'être à nous qui nous modifie intérieurement, de façon que notre esprit ou plutôt notre sensibilité intellectuelle reçoive ou non, plus ou moins ... et plus ou moins à la fois, et pendant plus ou moins longtemps à la fois, certaines impressions qui, séparées, ne donnent rien.[1]

The poet would wait for the impressions which, joined together at the right time, would produce some new idea or poetic *trouvaille*. There is still something of the Monsieur Teste in Valéry. The ambition of a "science autonome du mental"[2] may have faded, but the nostalgia is still there. Such an internal mechanism remains an ideal. But in fact, though control is indirect and tentative, the poet does, during his experience of 'exalted inspiration', achieve an adjustment and a timing not far removed from those of the perfect mechanism indicated. We saw that, in this state, Valéry thinks words are subject to laws and combinations quite different from those characterizing ordinary states of mind and body. There is, as it were,

un dictionnaire range de façon fortuite dont la *disponibilité* croit avec l'excitation. Une espèce de chaleur croissante détache en quelque sorte de parois les éléments verbaux, les agite et les rend dociles aux moindres appels—comme si leur inertie était diminuée. Leur excitabilité propre est prodigieusement accrue—Mobilité'.[3]

(This is as near as he gets to admitting that new associations depend on states of feeling. The images, particularly that of the "walls" from which the "verbal elements" become detached, adumbrate a rather antiquated psychology). It is to be noted that the state of 'exalted inspiration', particularly in the form of 'improvisation de degré supérieur', is not seen as reducible to formulae or rules which can be transmitted to be applied by another person; it is rather, in E. Noulet's phrase, "la

---

[1] *Cours de poétique* of 11 February 1938.
[2] Octave Nadal, in his introduction to the Valéry–Fourment correspondence, p. 31.
[3] *Cahiers, tome sixième*, p. 66.

transformation de l'intelligence en instinct," [1] a method made flesh and only so made by dint of long meditation, training and effort. Each poet has to perform the task for himself. These qualifications do not alter the interest for us and the reality for the poet of this striving towards the ideal state where something like the internal mechanism indicated does exist.

A similar notion of limited but real control over the timing of mental associations is implicit in a comment on metaphors:

> X . . . voudrait faire croire qu'une métaphore est une communication du ciel. Une métaphore est *ce qui arrive* quand on *regarde de telle façon*, comme un éternuement est ce qui arrive quand on regarde un soleil. De quelle façon? Vous le sentez. Un jour, on saura peut-être le *dire* très précisément. Fais ceci et cela,—et voici toutes les métaphores du monde.[2]

The vagueness and chimerical nature of this statement are obvious. In fact, when Valéry comes to discuss the possibility of control over the formation of metaphors, his tone is more tentative. It is none the less certain that he is able to suggest a way in which the formation of metaphors can be controlled or arrived at 'artificially'. Enquiring how metaphors are formed, he tells us that

> elles se produisent par voie d'arrêt sur la route des possibilités,[3]

that path through the field of possibilities constituted by the nervous system which goes from the "moi instantané" to the "moi complet." If, at the seaside, we see a distant object, such as a ship, and are not able to see it clearly enough to recognize it as such, we may conclude that it is a cloud or reef. To say that a ship is a cloud or reef is a metaphor. Thus, says Valéry,

> cet objet peu distinct est producteur comme la sensation en général quand on l'arrête dans son évolution vers la précision

---

[1] E. Noulet, *Paul Valéry*, Bruxelles, Editions de l'oiseau bleu, 1927, p. 22.
[2] *Calepin d'un poète, Poésies*, p. 192.
[3] *Cours de poétique* of 12 March 1938.

finale et résolutoire. Et à chaque instant une erreur de ce genre dans nos perceptions nous met sur la voie d'une métaphore possible.[1]

A metaphor is an incomplete notation, defined by a certain generality, by the fact that it establishes a relationship between objects which do not in fact resemble each other if they are examined attentively and objectively. The reader, when he experiences the metaphor in the poem, derives enjoyment from the unexpected relationship which he has to imagine. The poet can form at least the beginning of a metaphor quite deliberately,

> par une opération en somme assez simple sur un objet déterminé, en supprimant quelque chose dans son apparence, en réduisant le nombre de caractéristiques qu'il détermine entièrement.

He thus reaches

> une sorte d'objet moindre, d'objet moins réel qui, lui, peut ressembler à beaucoup de choses.[2]

Valéry concludes that, as precision increases, potential variations diminish, and, returning to his preoccupation with the problem of adjustment and timing, he claims that the poet needs only to delay this movement towards precision and

> quelques possibilités qui, sans ce retard, eussent été inactives, seront excitées.[3]

The avoidance of precision may be a conscious operation on words as the poet plays with them on paper, or it may be something he learns to do, internally, so to speak, by preventing the initial sensation of the "moi instantané" from reaching the stage of the "moi complet," or, more practically and feasibly, by noting down as speedily as possible impressions which are as near as possible to the stage of the "moi instantané." The poet can then examine and exploit such impressions.[4]

[1] *Ibid.*   [2] *Ibid.*   [3] *Ibid.*
[4] Cf. L. J. Austin: "Chez Valéry, l'esprit critique était attentif à la

"Proliferation" is the term used by Valéry to describe his method of composition. Poetic creation for him is not simply the recording of an initial experience: it is also the exploitation of what the poet has already written so that new experiences, of thought and feeling, are thereby gained. At first, the poem proliferates within the framework of the "intimation" we have examined. It is not possible to give a comprehensive plan for the way this proliferation takes place at the start of the poem. The poet may be preoccupied predominantly with the sense of the few lines composed, and seek to justify that sense by adding lines before or after. It may be a proliferation which starts from a desire to find a rhyme that fits the lines already composed.[1] Valéry envisages a constant modification of the growing poem as the poet seeks to tighten the relationships between *fond* and *forme*. It is moreover to be assumed that there are different intensities, one might even say, different forms of "intimation." The original one is often very powerful and gives the general framework of the poem as well as an aura of possibilities 'round the corner' in the area surrounding the first lines set down. This initial state wears off, or perhaps one should say that nothing more is forthcoming from it. The poet experiences no more "intimation" until he has worked for a time, predominantly 'with his head', and until he has limited the area of possibilities before him, tightened the conditions up to a certain point where "intimation" reappears.[2] When Valéry writes that

---

naissance même des idées et des images qui surgissaient dans sa conscience: très souvent, on le voit noter rapidement deux ou trois solutions qui se présentaient à son esprit, et dont il voulait exploiter les possibilités" (*op. cit.,* Grenoble, Roissard, 1954).

[1] Cf. Valéry's formulation and arresting image in *Cahiers, tome sixième,* p. 66: "L'être *attend* ce qu'il veut—Il cherche à provoquer une suite soit à ce qui est déjà acquis, soit à l'espoir d'acquérir, si excité. Il est dans l'état de l'amant qui a commencé son acte."

[2] Cf. *Cahiers, tome sixième,* p. 570: "*Serrer la préparation jusqu'au vers, c'est le point capital, le secret.* A force de voir, entendre. Prévoir jusqu'à avoir dépassé et acquis l'événement mental. Mais entendre dans tel ton et mystère *conventionnels!* Quelle improbabilité!

un beau vers m'est donné . . . J'en fais d'autres au-dessous et
au-dessus; seulement ceux-là il faut les faire,[1]

he may refer to painstaking, largely cerebral searching for and
fitting together of lines of poetry, or he may refer to work in
the framework of "intimation." Inevitably, the poet may have
to 'start from cold' each day or each time he begins a period of
composition; inevitably, at certain times, he neither has a *lueur*
nor can he see his way out of a particular difficulty, a particular
impasse. Poetry composed in such states would be truly "faite"
in Valéry's sense. Yet, once again, he seems to make too sharp a
distinction between "vers donnés" and "vers faits," in that,
after a period of groping, the poet will often, consciously or
unconsciously, so limit the possibilities before him as regards
composition that the state of "intimation" will recur and
illumination will result, with more attendant "intimation:"
then the post-illumination process we have described, for a few
or for many lines of the poem, starts again. Valéry gives an
instance of how the conditions are tightened by a mainly
intellectual effort, with regard to the smallest of local problems,
one word, a rhyme probably:

Je cherche un mot (dit le poète) un mot qui soit:
féminin,
de deux syllabes,
contenant P ou F,
terminé par une muette,

"Pour cela il ne faut pas vouloir dire expressément telle chose. *C'est déjà
des mots avant le vers;* ils doivent venir en lui, par lui et presque après lui!".

When we write of 'tightening the conditions', we mean by *conditions*
various factors—such as harmony, the indissolubility of sound and sense,
the awareness of what has already been composed and of what may be
approriate at this point in the poem—which exercise the poet at the moment.

[1] *Trio pour Henri Mondor* (Alain: Duhamel: Valéry), Paris, 1939, sur les
Presses Gauthier-Villars. Pages not numbered. Cf. *Cahier B, T.Q. I,* p. 218:
"Il y a des vers qu'on *trouve.* Les autres on les *fait.* On perfectionne ceux
qu'on a *trouvés.* On 'naturalise' les autres. Double simulation en sens inverse
pour atteindre ce faux: la perfection."

et synonyme de brisure, désagrégation;
et pas savant, pas rare.
Six conditions—au moins![1]

This is easy to solve without "intimation;" it can be done 'with the head' alone (Jean Hytier thinks so too—he suggests *rupture, fracture;* one might add *fêlure*), but with more difficult instances, the poet would often need to wait for the mind to throw up the solution or for the solution to be reached by a prolonged series of approximations. When an illumination is the result of such "intimation," we should classify it as 'secondary intuitive inspiration' (Hytier labels it "inspiration provoquée" in opposition to an "inspiration spontanée," our 'primary intuitive inspiration').[2] Valéry is famous for his "vers calculés," but it is to be supposed that many, if not all, poets have composed by calculation, if to a lesser extent.[3]

The creation and discovery of "obstacles" is a characteristic feature of this third stage of composition. Valéry has a keen sense of the arbitrary nature of existence;[4] the consequence is

[1] *Autres Rhumbs, T.Q. II,* pp. 153, 154.   [2] Jean Hytier, *op. cit.,* p. 145.

[3] One instance now famous is that of Housman, recounted in his book *The Name and Nature of Poetry,* Cambridge, at the University Press, 1933, p. 50. He tells how inspiration would come to him during long walks after lunch. Referring to such "suggestions", he writes: "When I got home, I wrote them down, leaving gaps, and hoping that further inspiration might be forthcoming another day. Sometimes it was, if I took my walks in a receptive and expectant frame of mind; but sometimes the poem had to be taken in hand and completed by the brain, which was apt to be a matter of trouble and anxiety, involving trial and disappointment, and sometimes ending in failure. I happen to remember distinctly the genesis of the piece which stands last in my first volume. Two of the stanzas, I do not say which, came into my head, just as they are printed, while I was crossing the corner of Hampstead Heath between the Spaniard's Inn and the footpath to Temple Fortune. A third stanza came with a little coaxing after tea. One more was needed, but it did not come: I had to turn to and compose it myself, and that was a laborious business. I wrote it thirteen times, and it was more than a twelvemonth before I got it right."

[4] Cf. *Note et Digression, Vinci,* p. 47: "*tout cela est égal...* Toutes choses se substituent,—ne serait-ce pas la définition des *choses?*" Anything can be regarded as an object by Valéry's 'awareness'.

that, for him, in poetic composition as in life generally, "le premier obstacle à l'acte est l'absence d'obstacles." [1] Like Mallarmé, he was sensitive to the blank sheet of paper before him. He wrote to Henri Mondor:

> Rien . . . n'est plus agréable, à mon avis, que de travailler sur une ébauche qui nous force, sans doute, à réagir contre l'imperfection que nous sentons, et n'ayant plus à penser à remplir le 'vide papier' où siège le vertige du commencement. [2]

The function of the second stage, the illumination, is to give the necessary start, something firm to work on and from. Once the first line or lines have been set down (they will not necessarily, of course, be the first lines of the eventual poem and may be modified later), the poet's mind and sensibility, characterized, as Valéry constantly points out, by disorder and incoherence, have something to 'bite on'. From the beginning of the third stage, the poet finds other "obstacles" which will enable him to orientate himself within the field of possibilities (perhaps already restricted, let us remember, if, like Valéry when he began to compose Le Cimetière Marin, the poet has been able to obtain a general idea of the themes and structure). What are these obstacles? In the first place, they are the conventions about which Valéry wrote so often, stressing how he welcomes them as something which forms a resistance to the disorder of his "fonctionnement d'ensemble," conventions which exist for any poet—rhyme, rhythm, verse-form, etc. Valéry adds to these obstacles by making conventions of the various criteria which are implicit in his conception of "pure poetry," or at least, of poetry as creating an "état chantant." This is tantamount to saying that the most important of these added obstacles are the indissolubility of fond and forme, sound and sense,[3]

---

[1] Le Physique du livre, in Paul Bonet, p. 22.
[2] Quoted by Henri Mondor in Paul Valéry: LE CIMETIÈRE MARIN. INTRODUCTION d'Henri Mondor, GENÈSE DU POÈME par L. J. Austin, Grenoble, Roissard, 1954. Pages not numbered.
[3] This indissolubility, as we have seen, implies the embodiment of several

the vital necessity of the poem's appeal as sound or music, and as much density as possible.[1] These precepts, for all their generality, are for him very efficacious: he seeks very deliberately to achieve in his verse an intense concentration of those elements calculated, as we saw earlier, to foil the intellect's attempt to classify and to make the most direct appeal to the reader's organic functions. Beginning with a line or lines of verse which appeal largely for their "propriétés sensibles," Valéry inevitably comes to the point where the meaning of the lines composed takes on an increasingly greater importance in deciding how the poem is going to develop further. In the event, the meaning towards which he is drawn is, by his own confession, in his own "metaphysical field."[2] It would be curious if it were otherwise. The initial "fragment(s)" or "vers donnés," "intimation" and the principles deduced from his study of poetry and his notion of "pure poetry" provide the essential, which is

de s'opposer à la pensée, de lui créer des résistances et de se fixer des conditions pour se dégager de l'arbitraire désordonné par l'arbitraire explicite et bien limité. On se se donne ainsi l'illusion d'avancer vers la formation d'un 'objet' de consistance propre, qui se détache de son auteur bien nettement.[3]

He makes it quite clear that any given poet will have his own

---

meanings in a given word, phrase or line, but meanings which often converge to express simultaneously different aspects of the thing in question.

[1] Cf. *Cahiers, tome sixième*, p. 922: "Les uns font leur œuvre en suivant une sorte de programme. Ils ont un sujet qu'ils vivent et ils exécutent partie par partie.

"Les autres ont présentes des conditions comme l'harmonie, les surprises, la rigueur—et ils y sacrifient leur sujet et ils exécutent comme simultanément les parties. Ils se vivent eux-mêmes et se parcourent, le sujet servant de repère."

[2] *La Création artistique, Vues*, p. 287.

[3] *Fragments des mémoires d'un poème, Var. V*, p. 115.

ideal of poetry and therefore his own obstacles or conventions.[1] The greater the difficulty in abiding by his conventions, in satisfying the exigencies he has set himself, the more the poet has to work and strive and the greater the feeling of satisfaction and certainty he has when the solutions are found. The fact that many exigencies are satisfied by a particular line or particular lines gives a certain autonomous existence to them.

Il faut, en quelque manière, *honorer, considérer* les difficultés qui se présentent. Une difficulté est une lumière. Une difficulté insurmontable est un soleil.[2]

We can understand what he means when, after detailing how he conceived the general structure of his poem *Le Cimetière Marin*, he confides that "un assez long travail s'ensuivit." [3]

During the third stage, as we have seen, Valéry envisages the poet as still receiving illuminations ('secondary intuitive inspiration'), still benefiting at times from "vers donnés," but the main trait of composition is deliberate exploitation of language:

Je n'invoque que ce hasard qui fait le fond de tous les esprits; et puis, un travail opiniâtre qui est *contre* ce hasard même.[4]

The manuscripts of Valéry's poems which are available[5] reveal how he will note down a whole series of words or phrases which form a kind of fan of meanings covering a given poetic development he is considering. He will then explore the possibilities of all or several of these words and this may lead him to further discoveries and possibilities. All ideas are jotted down, as near the nascent stage as possible, and as quickly as

---

[1] *Ibid.*, p. 114: "Je trouve, sans doute, si peu de raisons *d'écrire*, qu'à tant faire qu'à s'y mettre, et à ne pas se contenter de sensations et d'idées qu'on échange avec soi-même, il faut tenir *écrire* pour un problème, se prendre d'une curiosité pour la forme, et s'exciter à quelque perfection. Chacun peut se définir la sienne; et les uns d'après un modèle; les autres, par des raisonnements qui leur appartiennent."

[2] *M.P.*, p. 25.   [3] *Au sujet du Cimetière Marin, Var. III*, p. 64.

[4] *Autres Rhumbs, T.Q. II*, p. 163.

[5] See the bibliography for Octave Nadal's edition of *La Jeune Parque* and L. J. Austin's analysis of *Le Cimetière Marin*.

possible, to be examined at leisure to discover whether they satisfy his criteria.

The effort of this stage is illuminated by his distinction between the way man works and the way nature works:

> La nature, dans son travail, ne distingue pas les détails de l'ensemble; mais pousse à la fois de toutes parts, s'enchaînant à elle-même, sans essais, sans retours, sans modèles, sans visée particulière, sans réserves; elle ne divise pas un projet de son exécution . . .[1]

In man's creation, there are two time-scales involved,

> dont l'un s'écoule dans le domaine du pur possible, au sein de la substance subtile qui peut imiter toutes choses et les combiner à l'infini entre elles.[2]

This scale of time is in man's mind and sensibility, his imagination. But for these psychic combinations to assume an existence for anyone other than the poet himself, the latter must pass from the first time-scale to the second, which is

> celui de la nature. Il contient, d'une certaine façon, le premier, et d'une autre façon, il est contenu en lui. Nos actes participent des deux. Le projet est bien séparé de l'acte, et l'acte, du résultat.[3]

The work of the third stage of poetic creation consists of an exchange between these two time-scales. The poet

> n'est pas confondu à la matière de son ouvrage, mais il va et revient de cette matière à son idée, de son esprit à son modèle, et il échange à chaque instant *ce qu'il veut* contre *ce qu'il peut*, et *ce qu'il peut* contre *ce qu'il obtient*.[4]

A state of near-perfect exchange is only obtained in that state of virtuosity, the "improvisation de degré supérieur," which comes after long meditation and practice. It follows that the

---

[1] *Eupalinos ou l'Architecte, Eupad.*, p. 157. [2] *Ibid.*, p. 158. [3] *Ibid.*
[4] *Petit discours aux peintres graveurs, P.S.L.* 1948, p. 111.

third stage calls for "un cruel effort de coordination dans l'exécution." [1]

Valéry put the problem of co-ordination in different terms when he wrote:

> Le Poète, sans le savoir,[2] se meut dans un ordre de relations et de transformations possibles, dont il ne perçoit ou ne poursuit que les effets momentanés et particuliers dans tel état de son opération intérieure.[3]

This is the problem that faced Valéry above all during the composition of La Jeune Parque, because of both its length and its complexity. The poet gives himself up to a particular section of the poem, to a particular problem; he resolves the problem as best he can, though later he may modify the lines put down in the light of a comprehensive view of the poem, or a comprehensive view of a larger section than he had composed before. There are thus, to use Valéry's term, not only different "moments"[4] in that there are the three main stages, but also different "moments" within any stage, particularly the third.

The movement to and fro from one "moment" to another could not be better illustrated than with reference to the problem of the general direction the poem is to take at a given time. Valéry adheres to the precept laid down in Eupalinos:

> C'est qu'il m'importe sur toute chose, d'obtenir de ce qui va être, qu'il satisfasse, avec toute la vigueur de sa nouveauté, aux exigences raisonnables de ce qui a été.[5]

The principle is implicit in Valéry's notion of proliferation. But are we to understand the principle as applying to the poet at work, so that he keeps rigidly to the framework already

---

[1] Le Retour de Hollande, Var. II, p. 38.
[2] This unawareness would obviously seem to apply to other poets rather than to Valéry himself.
[3] Questions de poésie, Var. III, p. 46.
[4] La Création artistique, Vues, p. 306.
[5] Eupalinos ou l'Architecte, Eupad., p. 101.

adumbrated, or are we rather to interpret it as indicating the criteria which must be satisfied once any given lines are incorporated into a poem? For the young Valéry, the principle would appear to apply to the poet at work, following a fairly pre-determined path, so much so that Pierre Trahard, in his book, *Le Mystère poétique*, claims that for Poe and Valéry

> l'œuvre doit être tracée d'avance, selon un plan préconçu, et le poète ne peut s'en écarter, au risque de choir et de déchoir.[1]

What is true of the young Valéry is not true of the mature poet, who believes that "un poème ne se fait pas *à la suite*"[2] and also affirms:

> le poète ne peut pas dire, ne *doit* pas dire: je prends telle route pour aller là, je vise tel but. Il faut compter avec les surprises, les événements de mer, la dérive.[3]

During composition,

> l'esprit va, dans son travail, de *son* désordre à *son* ordre. Il importe qu'il se conserve jusqu'à la fin, des ressources de *désordre*, et que l'ordre qu'il a commencé de se donner ne le lie pas si complètement, ne lui soit pas un si rigide maître, qu'il ne puisse le changer et user de sa liberté initiale.[4]

Although for the mature Valéry a poem is still "un effet à produire,"[5] he surely, now, thinks that the principle formerly enunciated in *Eupalinos* applies only to the finished product, not to the poet at work; it is partly because the poet does not apply this principle to his explorations during composition that he is able the more effectively to make it apply to the finished

---

[1] Pierre Trahard, *Le Mystère poétique*, Paris, Boivin, Bibliothèque de la revue des cours et conférences, 1940.

[2] *L.Q.*, p. 145.

[3] Gabriel Audisio, *Première rencontre avec Paul Valéry*, *P.V.V.*, p. 177.

[4] *Analecta*, *T.Q. II*, pp. 228, 229.

[5] *P.V.V.*, p. 60.

poem, retrospectively.[1] If a line occurs to Valéry, an illumination or "vers donné" which is sufficiently brilliant and suggests many possibilities for the poem, he may find a place for it and modify his poem and the plan or framework he is working on at the moment,[2] depending, of course, on how far he has progressed with his poem. The further he has gone, the greater the number of exigencies which the purely inspired line will have to satisfy. This procedure is common to many poets and creative writers, for, as Rudolf Arnheim explains in *Poets at Work*,

> experiences in the psychology of thinking suggest that there will be dead-ends, new starts, movements of almost blind searching, and many instances of a dramatic 'restructuring' of the whole.[3]

The same variety of "moments" is evident in the question of *fond* and *forme*. We know that, according to Valéry, the poet sometimes has an idea to express and he must give it form; sometimes he has a certain form necessary for the poem which will decide the sense. The direction sense to form, as we saw, never seems to have been Valéry's experience during the second stage of creation, but it is certain that during the third stage he must often have had, if only from the lines already written, an idea, a sense to express. In fact, even during the third stage, the direction form to sense seems to have been at least as common for Valéry as the other. Thus he writes that

> une idée charmante, touchante, 'profondément humaine' (comme disent les ânes) vient quelquefois du besoin de lier deux strophes, deux développements. Il fallait jeter un pont, ou tisser des fils qui assurassent la suite du poème; et comme la suite toujours possible est l'homme même, ce besoin *formel* trouve une réponse—fortuite et heureuse chez l'auteur—qui

---

[1] Cf. L. J. Austin, *op. cit.* (Grenoble, Roissard, 1954).

[2] In a succinct sentence in *Cahiers, tome sixième*, p. 498, Valéry describes the poet as "préférant toujours à la volonté particulière de faire telle chose, sa volonté générale de faire une belle chose."

[3] *Op. cit.*, p. 136.

ne s'attendait pas de la trouver,—et *vivante*, une fois mise en place, pour le lecteur.[1]

He dreamed, more in his youth than in his maturity, of

la création d'ouvrages, à partir de conditions de forme, et presque par le seul assemblage de telles obligations de faire et de ne pas faire . . .[2]

He would determine the structure of the poem, its theme or themes, its verse-form, its various modulations and sections with their interrelations, abiding by his belief in density and indissolubility of sound and sense, and thus arriving at the rhymes and actual lines . . . This dream was not realized, on his own admission,[3] but the tendency to determine the sense by the form is still very present in the mature Valéry. It is probably at its strongest during the composition of *La Jeune Parque*. About the writing of this poem, he relates:

Il m'arrivait souvent de déterminer ce que les philosophes appellent, bien ou mal, le 'contenu' de la pensée (il vaudrait mieux parler du contenu des expressions) par des considérations de forme. Je prenais, si l'on veut, la pensée pour 'inconnue', et, par autant d'approximations qu'il en fallait, je m'avançais de proche en proche vers 'elle'.[4]

The method worked well on the whole, but he would be blind who did not see that, at times, the concern with form is too evident in *La Jeune Parque*, and that, in certain lines, Valéry does not get near enough to "pensée." The "poetic pendulum"[5] can be too much on the side of sound.[6] We can conclude, then,

---

[1] *Rhumbs, T.Q. II*, p. 76. Cf. *Cahier B, T.Q. I*, p. 203: "Il y a bien plus de chance pour qu'une rime procure une 'idée' (littéraire) que pour trouver la rime à partir de l'idée. Là-dessus repose toute la poésie et particulièrement celle des années 60 à 80."

[2] *Histoire d'Amphion, P.S.L.* 1948, p. 79.   [3] *Ibid.*   [4] *Mél.*, p. 42.

[5] *Poésie et pensée abstraite, Var. V*, p. 152.

[6] Cf. line twenty-five of *La Jeune Parque*

. . . "sur l'écueil mordu par la merveille".

The last word 'refers' presumably to the sea. It has been too obviously chosen for the rhyme and the alliteration.

that there are many different "moments" in the third stage, the poet working from *forme* to *fond*, from *fond* to *forme*, by illumination, 'primary intuitive' or 'secondary intuitive inspiration', or by an activity which is predominantly cerebral. The comprehensive view the poet must make might be considered as another "moment." It is one which must occur fairly frequently. The process is repeated and will embrace an ever increasing number of lines. Valéry gave instances of the way in which this led him to modify what had already been written. Of *La Jeune Parque* he wrote:

> J'ai été forcé, pour *attendrir* un peu le poème, d'y introduire des morceaux non prévus et faits après coup. Tout ce qui est sexuel est surajouté. Tel le passage central sur le Printemps qui semble maintenant d'importance essentielle.[1]

The particular *vue d'ensemble* which occasioned this modification seems to have occurred at a very late stage of composition. It should moreover be noted that this kind of viewpoint will often confirm in a quite conclusive manner what had been accepted provisionally at the time of discovery. Thus, though Pierre Louÿs did not like the words "transparente mort" in *La Jeune Parque*, Valéry explained why he insisted on keeping them in:

> Ici, j'avoue insister. Cette épithète se lie au passage précédent et à l'esprit général (trouvé après coup) du poème.[2]

When Valéry first found the phrase (easily or with effort, we do not know), he doubtless looked upon it as little more than a bringing together of syllables which fitted for sound and meaning into a small group of lines. He observed with acuity that

---

[1] *L.Q.*, p. 124. We find it difficult, if not impossible, to believe that the second sentence of this quotation is to be taken as applying to every sexual reference or implication in the poem. It seems that Valéry is referring to those parts which are, so to speak, concentratedly sexual.

[2] *Quinze lettres de Paul Valéry à Pierre Louÿs, lettre H.*

toute reprise consciente d'une idée la renouvelle; modifie, enrichit, simplifie ou détruit ce qu'elle reprend; et si même, dans ce retour, on ne trouve rien à changer dans ce que l'on avait une fois pensé, ce jugement qui approuve et conserve une certaine chose acquise, forme avec elle un fait qui ne s'était pas encore produit, un événement inédit.[1]

The phrase "l'esprit général (trouvé après coup) du poème," which is not so startling as it appears at first sight, in the light of the preoccupations already examined, confirms the importance of the comprehensive viewpoint, particularly when it is a question of a poem as long and as complex as *La Jeune Parque*. This poem was composed in sections, "îles," which must each have been subject to various *vues d'ensemble* and which had their "esprit général." The predominant tone of the poem as a whole was worked towards as Valéry sought to link the various sections (not so disparate as his comment might lead us to suppose) in one supreme perspective, which involved various modifications and much effort. "Les transitions m'ont coûté une peine infinie," [2] he wrote.

*

The third stage is essentially "un travail nécessairement discontinu." [3] Valéry defines it elsewhere as

une transaction, une mise en place, une subordination plus ou moins bien réussies de . . . conditions indépendantes,[4]

and speaks of the "diversité 'hétérogène' des conditions qui s'imposent." [5] But he gives us to understand that this work of compromise is not always done coldly and purely cerebrally. Roger Callois, whose gift for happy description we have already noted, defines one aspect of the poet's inspiration as "l'effervescence produite en lui par son travail." [6] Most poets,

---

[1] *Fragments des mémoires d'un poème, Var. V*, p. 113.   [2] *L.Q.*, p. 145.
[3] *Fragments des mémoires d'un poème, Var. V*, p. 115.
[4] *La Création artistique, Vues*, p. 298.   [5] *Ibid.*, p. 299.
[6] R. Callois, *op. cit.*, p. 51.

quite simply most writers, even writers of critical works, are well acquainted with this state—a form of 'exalted inspiration'. During the period of time covered by the third stage of creation, Valéry sees the poet as experiencing certain states —pleasurable tension, effort, analysis and waiting—which can be viewed as a unity:

> Un poète est, à mes yeux, un homme qui, à partir de tel incident, subit une transformation cachée. Il s'écarte de son état ordinaire de disponibilité générale, et je vois en lui se construire un agent, un système vivant producteur de vers.[1]

The "system" disappears when composition is abandoned: the poet in the man remains potential until another composition is begun.

During composition, the poet seeks to be very different from what he is ordinarily:

> Chacun de nous est en général très éloigné du point où le travail soutenu le mène. Travailleur, en ce sens, n'est-ce pas se contraindre à différer de soi?[2]

The poet, like a novelist such as Flaubert, wants to record only his finest moments, whether they are the result of illumination or of effort. The real unity behind all the diversity and heterogeneity of the third stage is provided by the evaluative faculty since it determines the use to which will be put the material resulting from these moments.[3] The notion of the presiding evaluative faculty is expanded and slightly changed by Valéry when, preserving the idea of an overriding unity derived from 'awareness', he declares that

> une œuvre est faite par une multitude 'd'esprits' et d'événements—(ancêtres, états, hasards, écrivains antérieurs, etc.)—

[1] *Poésie et pensée abstraite*, *Var. V*, p. 148.

[2] *La Création artistique*, *Vues*, p. 295.

[3] Cf. L. J. Austin's cogent observation: "Pour Valéry, 'l'inspiration' ne devait jamais être qu'une 'matière', et le véritable génie poétique était pour lui la finesse et la sûreté du jugement qui présidait au choix et à la disposition de cette matière" (*op. cit.*, Grenoble, Roissard, 1954).

sous la direction de l'auteur. Ce dernier doit donc être un profond politique attaché à mettre d'accord ces larves et ces actions intellectuelles concurrentes.[1]

He would perhaps have been more accurate if he had said that the poet is able to harmonize the products of these various activities more often than the activities themselves.

Certain consequences follow from Valéry's ideas on poetic composition. The poem as seen in its published form is rarely composed very quickly. Given the cruel effort of co-ordination involved, given his poetic ideal and the "refusals" imposed by it, composition is often laboured and protracted. It is true, however, that the speed of writing quickens as the poet gets nearer to the "improvisation de degré supérieur," while much depends on how complex, how ambitious the particular poem being composed is. His claims that a poem is never finished for him are too well known to need mention here: they follow logically from his attitude to poetic creation, since "pure poetry" is an ideal he never completely attained. The third stage of creation is the most difficult and can be seen as being literally of indefinite duration.[2]

---

[1] *Littérature, T.Q. I,* pp. 175, 176.

[2] Cf. *Cahiers, tome huitième,* p. 773: "Une œuvre n'est jamais nécessairement *finie,* car celui qui l'a faite ne s'est jamais accompli, et la puissance et l'agilité qu'il en a tirées, lui confèrent précisément le don de l'améliorer, et ainsi de suite... *Il en retire de quoi l'effacer et la refaire*—C'est ainsi du moins qu'un artiste *libre* doit regarder les choses. Et il en vient à tenir pour œuvres satisfaisantes celles seulement qui lui ont appris quelque chose de plus."

CONCLUSION: 'PERSONAL INSPIRATION'

IT is clear to the reader of Valéry's verse how much of himself he puts into it, despite its admirable control and impersonality. His poems are about his own life and thought, the *splendeurs et misères* of a certain kind of intellectual, ranging from the "comédie de l'intellect," that anguish and ecstasy of 'awareness' which find expression in poems such as *La Jeune Parque* or *Le Cimetière Marin*, to the theme of poetic composition in many of the poems of *Charmes*.[1] The controlled concentration of sound and sense, the tones of his poetry—exalted, sardonic, sombre, wistful, flippant, ironic, to mention a few—are, like the themes, an integral part of this self-expression. He was not usually eager to admit to what extent his most intimate preoccupations passed into his verse. He was not given to discussing very often what his poems were 'about'; this is understandable if we recall his views on the relationship between sense and form in poetry and his dismissal of the sense of a poem such as *La Jeune Parque* as 'commonplaces'.[2] But he nevertheless explained with care on several occasions what was 'in his mind' when he wrote certain poems;[3] and an excellent idea can thereby be formed of the original and personal contribution he wanted to make and did make to French poetry. Referring to the "amateur de l'esprit" whose taste in verse he is discussing, he explains:

[1] This is, of course, only a general description of the range of preoccupations to be found in his poetry. Many of the particular themes come within this range—for example, one of the main themes of *Ebauche d'un serpent*, in *Charmes*, is that of God and of "la contradiction fondamentale entre sa qualité d'Etre parfait et son acte de Créateur" (*Cahiers, tome sixième*, p. 434).

[2] "Le fond importe peu. Lieux communs. La vraie pensée n'est pas adaptable au vers" (*Lettre à André Fontainas, Réponses*, p. 16). He referred to the *fond* of his poems as "leur aspect 'mythique'." (*Fragments des mémoires d'un poème, Var. V*, p. 105).

[3] See particularly *Au sujet du Cimetière Marin* (*Var. III*), *Commentaires de Charmes* (*Var. III*), *Fragments des mémoires d'un poème* (*Var. V*), and *Le Prince et la Jeune Parque* (*Var. V*).

Et il lui arrive alors de prétendre . . . que la vie de l'intellect constitue un univers lyrique incomparable, un drame complet, où ne manquent ni l'aventure, ni les passions, ni la douleur (qui s'y trouve d'une essence toute particulière), ni le comique, ni rien d'humain. Il proteste qu'il existe un immense domaine de la sensibilité intellectuelle, sous des apparences parfois si dépouillées des attraits ordinaires que la plupart s'en éloignent comme de réserves d'ennui et de promesses de pénible contention. Ce monde de la pensée, où l'on entrevoit la pensée de la pensée et qui s'étend depuis le mystère central de la conscience jusqu'à l'étendue lumineuse où s'excite la folie de la clarté, est aussi varié, aussi émouvant, aussi surprenant par les coups de théâtre et l'intervention du hasard, aussi admirable par soi-même, que le monde de la vie affective dominé par les seuls instincts.[1]

Valéry had, and revealed in his poetry, an unequalled sensitivity concerning things intellectual, both in themselves and in their relationship with the body and with the external world.

The mature Valéry not only gave an excellent general characterization of his 'personal inspiration'; he also showed his awareness of the need for inspiration at this level in any poet. Particularly towards the end of his life, he seems to have grown very conscious of its importance, which we saw him utterly deny at the end of his *Introduction à la méthode de Léonard de Vinci* in 1896. Thus, in 1938, he asserted that

une œuvre d'art implique toujours une sorte d'inégalité, une sorte de parti pris et on pourrait appliquer au philosophe [2] la formule qui servait à l'école naturaliste: la nature vue à travers un tempérament.[3]

He made much in his later years of the egotism of the artist or philosopher: poetry, like any art, can be seen as the concentration of a certain *moi*. Just as, in Valéry's view

---

[1] *Descartes, Var. IV*, p. 215. Cf. also *La Création artistique, Vues*, pp. 286–288.
[2] *I.e.*, the philosopher seen as an artist.
[3] *Cours de poétique* of 5 February 1938.

le désir véritable de Descartes ne pouvait être que de porter au plus haut point ce qu'il trouvait en soi de plus fort et de susceptible de généralisation,[1]

so, he implies, all great men have something which is inalienably theirs, their precious originality. This must be preserved at all costs. If we apply the following sentence to Valéry himself, or to the poet, are we not near a definition of 'personal inspiration'?:

> il est possible, après tout, que l'être destiné à la grandeur doive se rendre sourd, aveugle, insensible à tout ce qui, même vérités, même réalités, traverserait son impulsion, son destin, sa voie de croissance, sa lumière, sa ligne d'univers.[2]

Perhaps the most striking evidence of his acceptance of 'personal inspiration' is the following passage from a conversation in 1943 with Lucien Fabre: the language is as significant as the thought:

> Je sais tout ce que je dois à Mallarmé et pour la conception de l'art et pour la technique et pour le vocabulaire. Pourtant, il est allé au bout de sa pensée et de son univers en un lieu où je ne pouvais pas le suivre parce qu'il y était porté par la *forme* même de ses propres ondes, par son *timbre* propre qui n'étaient pas les miens. Il n'est spécifiquement Mallarmé que là. Un poète n'est vraiment lui-même, n'est le *vrai* poète qu'à partir du moment où il ne s'agit plus pour lui des techniques ou des matières poétiques, (même inventées par lui dès lors qu'elles entrent dans le fonds commun), mais de sa qualité propre qui est *incommunicable.*[3]

The poet must bring to composition a personal contribution which, Valéry clearly indicates here, is not reducible to rules, analysis or conscious technique.

★

[1] *Une Vue de Descartes, Var. V*, p. 251.   [2] *Descartes, Var. IV*, p. 230.
[3] *P.V.V.*, p. 164.

Let us sum up his attitude to the various forms of inspiration we have distinguished. 'Total inspiration' was always rejected by him, both for his own purposes as a poet and, theoretically, for all poets. In the last analysis, this rejection appears well founded. 'Intermittent inspiration', the "poetic state," is fully analysed only by the mature Valéry. His experience seems to resemble that of the majority of poets; it is by his attitude towards the "poetic state"—his attempt to understand and control it—that he belongs to a minority. Concerning 'intuitive inspiration', his views, as we have noted, changed markedly. As a young man, he rejected it; in later life, he admitted it. Analysis led him to discover two forms of it and to exhibit clearly its connection with the stages of preparation and of composition. Once again, it appears that Valéry is simply being more articulate than other poets concerning a form of inspiration known to most of them. The theme of 'exalted inspiration' finds no place in his early theories; after *la Jeune Parque*, he describes it with masterly knowledge and it is dearer to him the older he becomes. 'Attributed inspiration', involving a value-judgement, is perhaps present by implication in the earlier theories, but it is only in later years that he analyses it convincingly. His contribution here is among the most original he made to our subject since, whatever qualifications one might wish to make about the importance of inspiration of this kind, his findings bring in value-judgement as an essential new factor and introduce a clarity which had been lacking in previous discussions. 'Personal inspiration', we have seen, is rejected by the young iconoclast, and is given considerable emphasis by the older poet.

In his youth, Valéry's claims for technique are very great, even extravagant: they do not convince largely because they are not supported by sufficient explanations and details. In these years, technique (all that is implied by 'awareness' and knowledge of the *métier*) is opposed to inspiration, the aspects of which are not differentiated as they are later in his life. In maturity, his claims for technique are smaller, more subtly formulated, and, given his explanations, much more convincing; despite the continuing desire for consciousness and control, technique is now usually seen as complementary to inspiration. Delacroix wrote:

> Technique et inspiration s'opposent, s'appellent, se supposent.[1]

This sentence, in its progression, summarizes excellently the chronological sequence of Valéry's findings.

It is noteworthy that he does not really reveal much of his technique in a narrow sense—as defined, for instance, by Jean Hytier: "les problèmes d'expression, de métrique, de musique verbale."[2] Hytier regrets the lacuna, as does Jean Ballard, who wrote that

> si on le questionnait sur sa ou ses techniques, il éludait le plus souvent le sujet, évitant de se mettre en scène.[3]

Various reasons can be adduced which, if they do not justify this omission, perhaps explain it. Valéry believed, as we have seen, that the enjoyment of many readers is fullest when they are in relative ignorance of the poet's means. Thus Hytier explains the omission by suggesting that Valéry simply did not wish to disclose the secrets of his poetic method.[4] He had an innate reserve and pride which inclined him to shun too obvious self-revelation. The motto *Cache ton dieu* had his approval. He liked to think of himself—with much justification—as being intellectually ahead of other men, alone and discovering new facts by analysis and introspection. It is, then, understandable, if not condonable, that he always showed some contempt for the critic, the reader and for literature itself. A certain mystification was perhaps not quite foreign to his silence about his technique in verse. Above all, he was aware of the immense difficulties inherent in any attempt to explain further than he did:

> Ce n'est que dans un nombre de cas infiniment faible que l'état mental peut se raconter.[5]

---

[1] Quoted by André Spire, *op. cit.*, p. 3.   [2] Hytier, *op. cit.*, p. 20.
[3] *P.V.V.*, p. 244.   [4] Hytier, *op. cit.*, p. 20.   [5] *L.Q.*, p. 51.

To repair the omission would have required much time and perhaps too much space. He usually preferred saying too little to saying too much.

Valéry knew that his poetry appealed to a necessarily limited audience. It could be claimed that, like his poetry, and for similar reasons, his views on inspiration and technique have an equally limited appeal, and indeed, a limited validity. His theories, some would argue, are based on too narrow and personal a conception of poetry; they reflect the inhibiting and extreme intellectualism of their author. His preoccupation with the intellect is the corner-stone of his ethics and of his aesthetics. Men, he thinks, have a morality because they have mental "thresholds," with consequent euphoria occasioned by sensibility. Beauty is that which attracts and which nevertheless cannot be defined and classified by the intellect; in poetry, the intellect must be appealed to, but the poet must organize his verse so that the mental "thresholds" will prevent classification and enable sensibility to create the desirable euphoria. The intellectual bias is too great. There are other things besides the intellect to be taken into account. Such theories, the argument would run, may be valid as far as his own composition is concerned; they are much less valid for poetry in general, which does not present such an appearance of cerebration, density and control and is not usually composed so consciously.

Valéry's considerable knowledge of modern discoveries and speculations in science and mathematics, as well as their importance for him in the exploration of his thought (particularly in his notebooks), would perhaps lead us to see him, in certain respects, as a man of the twentieth century. In other respects, however, it is not to our age that he seems to belong. Despite his constant awareness, especially in later years, of the interrelation of mind and body, he was perhaps too imprisoned by his basic acceptance of the two entities—in a manner uncharacteristic of our century. This was perhaps inevitable to the extent that psychology and psychiatry were still in their infancy during Valéry's most vital years as a thinker. He was clearly conscious of the dynamism inherent in poetic creation and could see it as an organic process. But when he analysed the "fonctionnement d'ensemble" he often used expressions which recall an obsolete psychology; he could lead his reader to believe that, for him, ideas are only fainter replicas of sense impressions and that poetic creation is merely an operation whereby certain *things* (ideas, impressions) are re-arranged according to certain laws of mental association. He sheltered too often and too easily behind his schematic distinction: intellect ("esprit," "conscience") and sensibility.[1] One sympathizes with his desire to comprehend under a word so general as sensibility all that is related to the emotive, affective, physiological and more or less unconscious side of our being. The fact remains that the word is too general. More precision was needed; with its help, he might have been enabled to acknowledge more fully and define more clearly the rôle of feeling and mood in poetic composition.[2] We are led to wonder why he did not exploit more the concept of imagination.[3] Another respect in which he is not a characteristic twentieth-century thinker is in the values he chose to uphold: clarity, 'awareness' and control. His advocacy of these virtues, his distrust of inspiration and "les choses vagues" no doubt have personal origins, but his distrust was perhaps made all the keener by his growing realization that the values he prized were of diminishing importance in modern society and particularly among many artists and poets.[4] Dadaism and

---

[1] This is true, we think, even though he coined terms—"sensibilité intellectuelle," "sensibilité généralisée"—which were meant to cover not only the senses and the emotions, but to some extent the workings of the intellect as well.

[2] It is worth noting that, in more than one *cours de poétique*, he dismissed the notion of the *subconscious* as too vague and naïve.

[3] In fact, he distrusted the notion. He tended to try to break it down into more analysable components—memory, invention, mental associations etc. Perhaps *imagination* was too dynamic, too uncontrollable and too unanalysable a concept to satisfy him. Some of his critics would probably claim that he did not have much imagination in the usual poetic sense.

[4] Cf. *Cahiers, tome cinquième*, p. 319: "Modernes. Les idées modernes de tachisme, 'harmonies', tout fonder sur des contrastes simultanés, négliger les suites, les développements, le dessin, se rapportent bien à l'état des idées.

surrealism, once he had recognized them for what they were, seem to have created a certain reaction in him. He became a torch-bearer for an attitude to life and art which has been eloquently discussed by Norman Suckling in his *Paul Valéry and the Civilized Mind*. It is one of literature's oddities that Baudelaire should have been the progenitor of both surrealism and Valéry.

But it is precisely because he carries further tendencies present in certain poets that he has much that is worthwhile to reveal. While disclosing a method which is his own, he is able, through the 'awareness' implicit in that method, to enlighten us not only about his own poetic composition but also about the problems of composition for any poet. He gives us the fruits of his powerful analysis, his clear and profound views of the whole field of literature and poetry, the relationship between poet and reader, the stages of poetic creation and the degree of consciousness and will which can be annexed to the commonly unconscious cultivation of the poet's character and the poetic act. One is struck by the contrast between the clumsy gropings of so many poets and theorists in the field which has concerned us and Valéry's frequently masterly touch, speaking as he does as poet, aesthetician and psychologist. He indicates the real but limited rôle of inspiration in all poets and its much more limited, but real, rôle in his own work.

To acknowledge the greatness of his ideal and his achievement in the pursuit of clarity and control does not entail being unaware of the bounds which even he inevitably encountered. As Roger Callois has cogently argued, expressing reservations to which Valéry's attitudes often give rise,

---

Cela revient à se borner à indiquer les *commencements*—l'état naissant.

"Le désir finit par remonter le cours des événements psychophysiologiques et par essayer de fixer les seuls premiers termes... Ceux antérieurs même à l'impression photographique.

"On demande donc à l'artiste, *sensibilité* avant tout. Il n'est plus question d'habileté—On lui fait faire demi-tour pour en obtenir non plus quelque chose de *plus* que ce que tout le monde voit mais qq. chose de *moins*."

on conçoit sans peine comment une conscience attentive prémédite l'architecture d'un tableau, d'un sonnet ou d'une fugue. Elle sait évidemment combiner avec sûreté les couleurs, les rythmes, les sons, provoquer un besoin pour le combler ensuite, composer la surprise et l'attente, établir les moyens convenables à chaque fin et, par tout un concours d'amorces, de rappels, de progrès étudiés, faire de l'œuvre une joie perpétuelle pour l'esprit et les sens. Mais cette adresse, pour consommée qu'on l'imagine, n'est que régulatrice. Elle administre des richesses qu'elle reste impuissante à produire ... Je ne vois pas que l'intelligence crée jamais la matière qu'elle s'efforce d'organiser, ni la volonté le but où elle décide de tendre. L'une et l'autre ne sont qu'instruments.[1]

When Valéry asserts that

une œuvre exprime non l'*être* d'un auteur, mais sa *volonté de paraître*, qui choisit, ordonne, accorde, masque, exagère,[2]

it is readily appreciated that he is reacting against a certain kind of biographical criticism; but, in fact, the artist's work necessarily reveals and expresses both his *être* and his *volonté de paraître*. Once again, we have occasion to note how Valéry tends to falsify a truth by overstating it. On another occasion, the point that we have just seen him make is rephrased and depends for its force on the ambiguity of the word *soi*:

Chacun de nous est en général très éloigné du point où le travail soutenu parfois le mène. Travailler, en ce sens, n'est-ce pas se contraindre à différer de soi?[3]

The point is a valid and an excellent one, as we have seen, but it is overstated, no doubt deliberately, in that he is tending to make too sharp a distinction between the 'ordinary' self and the self of the composing artist. The too trenchant distinction between the *être* and the *volonté de paraître* of the poet, and the

---

[1] R. Callois, *op. cit.*, p. 54.   [2] *Une Vue de Descartes, Var. V*, p. 220.
[3] *La Création artistique, Vues*, p. 295.

implication that the former does not have anything like the same importance in creation as the latter, are at variance with his own statements on what we have called 'personal inspiration'.

One of the most recent developments in Valéry criticism [1] is to stress the continuity of his preoccupations in the 1890s and in the second decade, and after, of the twentieth century. The clear demarcation between Valéry the poet and the Valéry of Maurice Bémol's "Grand Silence" is slowly vanishing. The following letter to Gide in 1891, particularly the last sentence, seems to corroborate this notion of continuity:

> J'ai galopé sur toutes les routes, crié l'appel sur tous les horizons. Un coin de ma vie passée—inconnue à jamais à Tous [2]—m'a éclairé sur le battement de la petite bête. Sensualité exaspérée. La science m'a ennuyé, la forêt mystique ne m'a conduit à rien, j'ai visité le navire et la cathédrale, j'ai lu le plus merveilleux Poe, Rimbaud, [3] Mallarmé, analysé, hélas! leurs moyens, et toujours j'ai rencontré les plus belles *illusions*, à leur point de genèse et d'enfantement. Où trouverais-je une magie plus neuve? Un secret d'être et de créer qui me surprenne? Tu souriras, ici, en songeant à mes pauvres essais? Si tu savais combien—réellement—je les déteste. Mes grands poèmes cherchent leur forme, et c'est insensé! [4]

A great deal was needed for his poems to find their form: perhaps, more than anything, a change of attitude as the gulf

---

[1] See particularly Octave Nadal's introduction to the Valéry–Fourment correspondence, *op. cit.*

[2] Valéry was fortunately mistaken here. He is referring to the episode of *la belle Catalane* with whom he fell in love. See H. Mondor, *Les Premiers temps d'une amitié—André Gide et Paul Valéry*, Monaco, Editions du Rocher, 1947, p. 157, and Octave Nadal, *Paul Valéry et l'événement de 1892, Mercure de France*, 1 April 1955, as well as certain letters and Nadal's introduction in his edition of the Valéry–Fourment correspondence.

[3] The quotation reveals only too clearly the influence of Rimbaud, especially in the first sentence.

[4] *L'Arche*, October 1945, p. 20.

between reality and the self became more painfully apparent to him. This change of attitude is as important as the change which took place in the early 1890s, though probably much more gradual. Moreover, this change of attitude and the poetry which resulted from it would not have been possible without the period from 1892 to 1913, and the thought, analysis, preparation and general equipment which were a product of it. He did not do what he did during these years with a view to poetic composition later in life: the fact remains, as he himself recognized, that "le démon ou le sens de l'art veillait au fond de [son] esprit." [1]

Thus, when all has been said on the various aspects of Valéry's thought which emphasize technique, control, clarity and 'awareness' in poetic composition, it remains that, of all the forms of inspiration available to him, his own 'personal inspiration' is perhaps the most important. He may have written that " 'l'inspiration' ne doit être qu'une matière," [2] but this observation presents only part of the truth. His poetry owes much of its greatness to his 'personal inspiration'. The fact has naturally been asserted by several critics.[3] Very bold

---

[1] *La Création artistique, Vues*, p. 286.

[2] *Fontaines de mémoire, P.S.L.* 1948, p. 247.

[3] Aimé Lafont, for instance, writes: "Que Valéry se crée des résistances, afin de dérouter son *Moi* souterrain qui veut paraître au jour; qu'il accepte les règles les plus inflexibles, qu'il se forge des chaînes, plus dures encore; le subconscient émergera malgré tout, et, pour nous servir de ses propres comparaisons, l'ingénieur pourra capter la source, la canaliser, la répandre en jets et jeux multiples, il n'en changera pas la qualité, et l'eau recueillie dans un vase donnera à l'analyse de sûrs renseignements sur son origine et les couches de terrains qu'elle a traversés" (*Paul Valéry: l'homme et l'œuvre*, Marseille, Jean Vigneau, 1943, p. 178). Marcel Raymond echoes Lafont: "le poète pourra bien s'imaginer qu'il choisit en toute lucidité l'ordre de ses pensées, les images, le mètre, tous les éléments constitutifs de son chant: néanmoins, une profonde 'aura', inséparable de son sentiment de l'existence, passera dans son langage, peut-être à son insu, peut-être incognito [The last words might appear to be true from many statements made by Valéry, when he is stressing control and consciousness, but they are not true in the light of the awareness he showed of 'personal inspiration']. En un mot, Valéry a beau vouloir ne s'avouer présent que dans l'acte de faire, son poème, saisi dans la totalité de ses harmoniques, ne se conçoit pas indépen-

in its delicacy and charm is a comment of Saint-Exupéry which might be applied to Valéry:

> Le théoricien ... croit mépriser le rêve, l'intuition et la poésie. Il ne voit pas qu'elles se sont déguisées, ces trois fées, pour le séduire comme un amoureux de quinze ans. Il ne sait pas qu'il leur doit ses plus belles trouvailles. Elles s'étaient présentées sous le nom 'd'hypothèses de travail', de 'conditions arbitraires', d' 'analogies', comment eût-il soupçonné, le théoricien, qu'il trompait la logique austère[1] et qu'en les écoutant il écoutait chanter les Muses...[2]

Could we class Valéry's beloved "conditions arbitraires," his well analysed "hypothèses de travail" as inspiration? From a certain point of view, they might be seen as an aspect of 'personal inspiration', because they form part of the inspiring principle which governed his particular kind of poetic composition; they were part of the means whereby he linked the two sides of his intellectual life,

> l'une toute vouée à l'étude passionnée et opiniâtre de quelques questions, qui, [il l'a] su plus tard, pouvaient être des questions de philosophe: l'autre, consacrée à quelque production littéraire (sous forme de poésie).[3]

We have conjectured that one of the factors which led him to return to full poetic creation in 1913 was the increasingly painful awareness of the gulf between reality and the self. His kind of analysis, by his own definition, is that which separates him from heterogeneous reality. A dilemma is reached as he tires of the task of analysis, which in the last resort proves ineffectual.[4] A superabundant, transcendent feeling of his own self overwhelms the poet:

---

damment des 'états de poésie' qui l'ont rendu possible" (*Paul Valéry ou la tentation de l'esprit*, Neuchâtel, A la Baconnière, 1946, p. 101).

[1] These last words, of course, would not apply to Valéry.

[2] *Un Sens à la vie*, Paris, Gallimard, 1956, p. 258.

[3] *La Création artistique*, *Vues*, p. 285.

[4] Analysis, that is, such as is found particularly in the notebooks.

Et, enfin, si le sentiment du *Moi* prend cette conscience et cette maîtrise centrale de nos pouvoirs, s'il se fait délibérément système de références du monde, foyer des réformes créatrices qu'il oppose à l'incohérence, à la multiplicité, à la complexité de ce monde aussi bien qu'à l'insuffisance des explications reçues, il se sent alimenté soi-même par une sensation inexprimable, devant laquelle les moyens du langage expirent, les similitudes ne valent plus, la volonté de connaître qui s'y dirige s'y absorbe et ne revient plus vers son origine, car il n'y a plus d'objet qui la réfléchisse. Ce n'est plus de la pensée . . .[1]

Valéry affirms that this plenitude of feeling is not expressible in language, but it is to be supposed that he means the language of analysis, or the language of poetry only when the feeling is at its most intense point; below this point, it would be expressible, and only expressible, in the language of poetry, that language which is both thought and emotion combined in such a way as to capture the plenitude and objectify it.[2] The kind of absolute which this plenitude of feeling represents is matched by the kind of absolute represented by the poem.[3]

It can thus be argued that poetry was experienced by Valéry as an authentic and satisfying mode of being.[4] He was a true

---

[1] *Descartes, Var. IV*, p. 230.

[2] Cf. Marcel Raymond, *op. cit.*, p. 109: "Par le moyen des objets, le poète aura le sentiment d'exprimer ces choses, ou cette chose très intime qu'il serait bien empêché d'atteindre jamais, et surtout de formuler, par les procédés habituels, si déliés soient-ils, de l'introspection. Cette chose fuit sous le scalpel, ou se dissipe en nuée sitôt que l'intellect la guette. Elle ne se laisse pas saisir, étant de l'ordre de la vie, qui est 'interdite à la pensée'. En revanche, elle consent à entrer dans une sorte de système de relation magique avec les objets. Le moins qu'on puisse croire, c'est que, sous un certain regard, l'ensemble de l'univers instant au poète, à un moment donné, se présente à lui comme un champ de virtualités expressives qui exigent de passer à l'acte, qui engendrent le besoin de la parole efficace et rémunératrice."

[3] As J. Wahl writes in *Sur la pensée de Paul Valéry*, in the *N.R.F.*, 1 September 1933, p. 456, the function of poetic creation is thus "dans un monde d'universelle relativité de créer un petit monde absolu."

[4] Valéry affirms of poetry in *Cahiers, tome sixième*, p. 906: "Elle a son *être* qui ne se résout pas finalement en *connaître*."

poet in that, through poetry, he achieved the transcendent union of self and reality which perhaps all poets seek, which the best convey, and which brings to them and to us, their readers, absorbing happiness.

BIBLIOGRAPHY

This bibliography, both for Valéry's works and others, gives only those mentioned in this study. We have referred where possible to the twelve-volume collection of Valéry's works given below. The collection is not complete and we have listed immediately afterwards the other publications mentioned.

Abbreviations, in brackets, are given for those works often quoted.

A. Works by Valéry

1. THE TWELVE-VOLUME COLLECTION

L'Ame et la Danse, Eupalinos ou l'Architecte, Paradoxe sur l'Architecte, (Eupad), Paris, Ed. du Sagittaire, 1931.

Monsieur Teste, La Soirée, le log-book, quelques épîtres, (Teste), Paris, Ed. du Sagittaire, 1931.

Album de vers anciens, La Jeune Parque, Charmes, Calepin d'un poète, (Poésies), Paris, Ed. de la N.R.F., 1933.

Variété, (Var. I), Paris, Ed. de la N.R.F., 1934.

Discours, Paris, Ed. de la N.R.F., 1935.

L'Idée fixe, ou deux hommes à la mer, Socrate et son médecin, (L'Idée fixe), Paris, Ed. de la N.R.F., 1936.

Variété, deuxième volume, (Var. II), Paris, Ed. de la N.R.F., 1937.

Pièces sur l'art, Degas, Danse, Dessin et divers écrits sur la peinture, (P.S.L.), Paris, Ed. de la N.R.F., 1938.

Les divers essais sur Léonard de Vinci, (Vinci), Paris, Ed. de la N.R.F., 1938.

Regards sur le monde actuel, (Regards), Paris, Ed. de la N.R.F., 1938.

Conférences, (Conf.), Paris, Ed. de la N.R.F., 1939.

Ecrits divers sur Stéphane Mallarmé, (Mall.), Paris, Ed. de la N.R.F., 1950.

2. WORKS WHICH SUPPLEMENT THE ABOVE COLLECTION

The first date given, in brackets, is the year the book appeared. At the end of each reference are given the new texts, if any, which have appeared in re-editions. The second date given, without brackets, indicates the edition which we have used. A mention in brackets after the second date indicates the abbreviation used in this study.

Variété, (1924), 1948, *(Var. 1948)*, Paris, Gallimard. *(Avant-propos pour la Connaissance de la Déesse de Lucien Fabre: Au sujet d'Eureka: Hommage à Marcel Proust)*.

Regards sur le monde actuel et autres essais, nouvelle édition revue et augmentée, (1931), 1945, *(Regards II)*, Paris, Gallimard. *(L'Amérique projection de l'esprit européen: Pensée et art français: Notre destin et les lettres: La Liberté de l'esprit: La France travaille: Métier d'homme: Coup d'œil sur les lettres françaises: Economie de guerre de l'esprit: Fonction et mystère de l'Académie).*

Monsieur Teste, (1931), 1950, (*Teste II*), nouvelle édition augmentée de fragments inédits, Paris, Gallimard. (*La Promenade avec Monsieur Teste: Pour un portrait de Monsieur Teste: Quelques pensées de Monsieur Teste: Fin de Monsieur Teste).*

Pièces sur l'art, (1934), 1948, (*P.S.L.* 1948), Paris, Gallimard. (*De l'éminente dignité des arts du feu: Broderies de Marie Monnier: Les deux vertus d'un livre: Livres: Lettre à Madame C...: Les Droits du poète sur la langue: Poèmes chinois: Au concert Lamoureux en 1893: La Conquête de l'ubiquité: Glose sur quelques peintures: Petit discours aux peintres graveurs: Regards sur la mer: L'Infini esthétique: Variations sur la céramique illustrée: Mon buste: Fontaines de mémoire).*

Variété III, (1936), 1949, (*Var. III*), Paris, Gallimard.

Variété IV, (1938), 1947, (*Var. IV*), Paris, Gallimard.

Variété V, (1944), 1948, (*Var. V*), Paris, Gallimard.

Mon Faust, (1946), 1949, Paris, Gallimard.

The article, *Sur la technique littéraire,* in *Le premier article de Paul Valéry,* pp. 13–30 of *Dossiers,* Paris, Janin, July 1946.

Vues, (1948), 1948, Paris, Janin, Collection le Choix de la Table Ronde.

Histoires brisées, (1950), 1950, Paris, Gallimard.

3. Notes and Anecdotes

Tel Quel I, (1941), 1948, (*T.Q. I*), Paris. Comprising *Choses tues* (1930), *Moralités* (1931), *Ebauches de pensées, Littérature* (1930) and *Cahier B 1910* (1930).

Mélange, (1941), 1943, (*Mél.*), Paris, Gallimard.

Mauvaises pensées et autres, (1942), 1942, (*M.P.*), Paris, Gallimard.

Tel Quel II, (1943), 1948, (*T.Q. II*), Paris, Gallimard. Comprising *Rhumbs* (1926), *Autres Rhumbs* (1927), *Analecta* (1926) and *Suite* (1934).

Propos me concernant, (1944), 1944, (*Propos*), in *Présence de Valéry,* by Berne-Joffroy, Paris, Plon.

Cahiers, Paris, Centre National de la Recherche Scientifique, *tomes I* (1957), *II* (1957), *III* (1958), *IV* (1958), *V* (1958), *VI* (1958), *VIII* (1959).

4. Other Writings

Quinze lettres de Paul Valéry à Pierre Louÿs (1915–1917), Paris, 1926.

Réponses, Paris, Au Pigeonnier, 1928.

Poésie (Essais sur la poétique et le poète), Paris, Collection Betrand Guégan, 1928.

Fragments de lettres inédites de Valéry à Paul Souday, in the *Catalogue de la bibliothèque de feu Monsieur Paul Souday,* Paris, George Andrieux, 1930.

Trio pour Henri Mondor (Alain: Duhamel: Valéry), Paris, Sur les presses Gauthier–Villars, 1939.

Esquisse d'un éloge de la virtuosité—introduction to *Paganini à Nice* by Louis Bonfiglio, publié par les soins de la ville de Nice, 27 May 1940.

Orient, by Pius Servien, followed by *Le Cas Servien* by Valéry, Dijon, Gallimard, 1942.

Le Physique du livre, in *Paul Bonet*, Paris, Auguste Blaizot, 1945.

Souvenirs poétiques, recueillis par un auditeur au cours d'une conférence prononcée à Bruxelles le 9 janvier 1947, Paris.

Lettres à Quelques-uns, (L.Q.), Paris, Gallimard, 1952.

Paul Valéry–Gustave Fourment. Correspondance (1887–1933), introduction, notes et documents par Octave Nadal, Paris, Gallimard, 1957.

5.   PREFACES WRITTEN BY VALÉRY

To *Coffrets Etoilés*, by André Lebey, Paris, La Connaissance du livre, 1918.

To *Papiers*, by Edouard Julia, Paris, Editions du Temps, 1936.

To *Les Carnets de Léonard de Vinci*, traduits de l'italien par Louis Servicen, Paris, Gallimard, 1948.

To *Les Chimères*, by Gérard de Nerval, Paris, Les Amis de la poésie, 1944.

To *Poèmes*, by Ladislas Mécs, Paris, Horizons de France, 1944.

B. Writings on Valéry mentioned in this book

Austin, L. J., *La Genèse du* CIMETIÈRE MARIN, Cahiers de l'Association internationale des Etudes françaises, July, 1953.

Austin, L. J., *Paul Valéry: LE CIMETIÈRE MARIN. INTRODUCTION d'Henri Mondor*, GENÈSE DU POÈME *par L. J. Austin*, Grenoble, Roissard, 1954.

Bémol, M., *Paul Valéry*, Paris, Les Belles Lettres, 1949.

Buchet, E., *Ecrivains intelligents du XXe siècle*, Paris, Corréa, 1945— pp. 127–168, *Paul Valéry et les limites de l'intelligence.*

Cain, L.-Julien, *L'Etre vivant selon Valéry*, in *La Nef* of March 1946, number 16.

Chardon, P., *Paul Valéry et la médecine*, Paris, Editions Armand Fleury, 1930.

Fernandat, R., *Autour de Paul Valéry*, Paris, Arthaud, 1944.

Fontainas, A., *De Mallarmé à Valéry (lettres et souvenirs inédits)*, in *La Revue de France* of 15 September 1927.

Gide, A., *Paul Valéry*, Paris, Collection Au Voilier, Domat, 1947.

Hytier, J., *La Poétique de Valéry*, Paris, Armand Colin, 1953.

Jones, R. S., *Poincaré and Valéry; a note on the 'symbol' in science and art*, in *Modern Language Review*, vol. XLII, no. 4, October 1947.

Lafont, A., *Paul Valéry, l'homme et l'œuvre*, Marseille, Jean Vigneau, 1943.

Latour, J. de, *Examen de Valéry, précédé d'une lettre et d'un texte inédits de Paul Valéry*, Paris, Gallimard, 1935.

Lefèvre, F., *Entretiens avec Paul Valéry*, Paris, Flammarion, 1926.

Mondor, H., *Vie de Mallarmé*, Paris, Gallimard, 1946.

Mondor, H., *Les premiers temps d'une amitié—André Gide et Paul Valéry*, Monaco, Editions du Rocher, 1947.

Nadal, O., edition of LA JEUNE PARQUE—*Manuscrit autographe, texte de l'édition de 1942, états successifs et brouillons inédits du poème. Présentation et étude critique des documents par Octave Nadal*, Paris, Le Club du meilleur livre, 1957.

Noulet, E., *Paul Valéry*, Bruxelles, Editions de l'oiseau bleu, 1927.

Noulet, E., *Paul Valéry (Etude), édition définitive*, Bruxelles, La Renaissance du livre, 1950.

Raymond, M., *Paul Valéry ou la tentation de l'esprit*, Neuchâtel, A la Baconnière, 1946.

Rideau, E., *Introduction à la pensée de Paul Valéry*, Paris, Desclée de Brouwer, 1944.

Scarfe, F., *The Art of Paul Valéry (A study in dramatic monologue)*, London, William Heinemann Ltd., Glasgow University Publications XCVII, 1954.

Suckling, N., *Paul Valéry and the Civilized Mind*, University of Durham publications, Oxford University Press, 1954.

Sutcliffe, F. E., *La Pensée de Paul Valéry. Essai*, Paris, Nizet, 1955.

Wahl, J., *Sur la pensee de Paul Valéry*, pp. 449–463 in *La Nouvelle Revue Francaise of* 1 September 1933.

Paul Valéry Vivant (P.V.V.), Les Cahiers du Sud, Marseille, 1946.

C. Other works mentioned

Abrams, M. H., *The Mirror and the Lamp : Romantic Theory and the Critical Tradition*, New York, Oxford University Press, 1953.

Arnheim, R., Auden, W. H., Shapiro, K., Struffnerm, D.A., *Poets at Work.* (Essays based on the modern poetry collection at the Lockwood Memorial Library, University of Buffalo), New York, Harcourt, Brace and Co., 1953.

Bowra, C. M., *Inspiration and Poetry* (Rede lecture delivered at Cambridge in 1951), London, Macmillan, 1955.

Callois, R., *Les Impostures de la poésie*, Paris, Gallimard, 1945.

Clark, Sir K., *Moments of Vision* (The Romanes Lecture), Oxford, Clarendon Press, 1954.

Coleridge, S. T., *Biographia Literaria*, London, Oxford University Press, 1949, two volumes.

Downey, J. E., *Creative Imagination* (Studies in the Psychology of Literature), London, Kegan Paul, Trench, Trubner and Co. Ltd., 1929.

Harding, R. E. M., *An Anatomy of Inspiration*, Cambridge, W. Heffer & Sons Ltd., 1948.

Housman, A. E., *The Name and Nature of Poetry*, Cambridge, at the University Press, 1933.

Poincaré, H., *La Valeur de la science*, Genève, Editions du cheval ailé,

Classiques français du XXe siècle, avec une introduction de Louis Rougier, Bourquin, 1946.

Poincaré, H., *Science et méthode*, Paris, Flammarion, 1947.

Read, Sir H., *Collected Essays in Literary Criticism*, Faber, 1938.

Ribot, Th., *Essai sur l'imagination créatrice*, Paris, Alcan, 1926.

Richards, I. A., *Coleridge on Imagination*, London, Routledge and Kegan Paul, 1934.

Saint-Exupéry, A. de, *Un Sens à la vie*, Paris, Gallimard, 1956.

Shelley, P. B., *A Defence of Poetry*, in *Shelley's Prose*, edited by D. L. Clark with an introduction and notes, Albuquerque, The University of New Mexico Press, 1954.

Skelton, R., *The Poetic Pattern*, London, Routledge and Kegan Paul, 1956.

Spire, A., *Plaisir poétique et plaisir musculaire, (Essai sur l'évolution des techniques poétiques)*, Paris, José Corti, 1949.

Trahard, P., *Le Mystère poétique*, Paris, Boivin, Bibliothèque de la revue des cours et conférences, 1940.

Wallas, G., *The Art of Thought*, London, C. A. Watts and Co. Ltd., 1945.

INDEX

Abrams, M. H., 1n
Absolute (noun), 21, 176
Abstract words and "aesthetic infinite", 85
Accommodation or adjustment, 50n, 60n, 130, 145–148
"Aesthetic infinite", 49n, 50, 71, 77–80, 82, 85, 87, 88
Ambiguity, 85, 86, 86n, 91n
Aristotle, 1
Arnheim, R., 140, 158
"Attente", 96, 117; see "intimation"
Auden, W. H., 140–141
Aurore, 116
Austin, L. J., 69, 76n, 94n, 137n, 142n, 148n, 154n, 158n, 162n
"Availability", 49, 50, 55, 86, 130, 162; see "cours naturel"
'Awareness', 26, 26n, 27, 35, 36, 51, 53, 62, 107, 126, 162, 164, 167, 170, 171, 174
Ayer, A. J., 60n

Ballard, J., 168
Baudelaire, 5, 76, 171
Bémol, M., 23n, 173
Bergson, 29
Blake, 3, 6, 32
Bowra, Sir Maurice, 8n, 105n, 113n, 133
Broglie, L. de, 28
'Buried stream' theory, 123, 125

Calculation, 11, 98, 104, 129–131
Callois, R., 132, 141, 142, 143, 161, 171
Carlyle, 4
Charmes, 31, 116, 131, 164
Cimetière Marin, Le, 68, 79, 128, 137, 142, 152, 154, 164
Clark, Sir Kenneth, 137n
Coleridge, 5, 8, 137

Collège de France, vii, 35, 62
Composition, (attitude towards) 64–69, 96, 108, 129–163
Condillac, 49
Conscious (-ness, -ly), 2, 3, 4, 6, 10, 11, 15, 17, 22, 24, 25, 31, 33, 38, 51, 58, 61, 62, 64, 66, 67, 76, 80n, 84, 95, 98, 99, 103, 105, 105n, 108, 117, 120, 121, 124, 125, 126, 130, 131, 133, 134, 134n, 135, 138, 139, 139n, 140, 140n, 141n, 142, 144, 148, 150, 165, 168, 170, 171, 172, 174n, 176; see 'awareness'.
Continu, le, continuity, 17, 22, 23, 23n, 28, 40, 97
Conventions in poetry, 152–154
Co-ordination(s), 43, 43n, 67, 99, 101n, 112, 156, 163
"Cours naturel, le," 55–56, 78, 79, 86, 87, 103, 106, 106n, 130

Dadaism, 170
Delacroix, 168
Descartes, 52, 166
Determinism, 53
Discontinu, le, discontinuity, 23, 23n, 28, 37, 43n, 143, 161
Downey, J. E., 48, 50n, 52, 108n, 137, 138
Dynamism, 4, 18, 169

Ebauche d'un serpent, 164n
Egotism of artist, 165
Einstein, 28
Eliot, T. S., 137
Empiricism, 33, 135
"Enchantement", 74, 76, 91
"Etats d'attente", 55, 144
Eupalinos, 157
Euphoria, 60, 90, 138, 169
Evaluative faculty, 72, 102, 103, 131, 162
Exaltation, states of, 75, 86, 103, 115

Fabre, L., 166
Feeling, 2, 3, 4, 62, 136–138, 146, 170
Flaubert, 162
"Fragments" of verse, 7, 33, 71, 95, 100, 102, 114, 115, 118, 153
French Studies, 21n
Fringe-consciousness, 139–140
Fringe-ideas, 136

Gallimard, 68, 116, 123, 125
Genius, 3, 4, 15, 17, 97, 103, 112n, 145
Gestalt psychology, 53
Gide, A., 65, 68, 116, 123, 125, 173
Graves, R., 134n
Grenades, Les, 137

Habit, 52–54, 55, 60, 106, 106n, 107
Harding, R., 108n, 136
Hazlitt, 3
Heisenberg, 28
Heredia, 5
Horatian tradition, 2
Housman, A. E., 134n, 151n
Hugo, 4
Hytier, J., 30, 32n, 41, 92n, 151, 168

Illumination, 7, 96, 96n, 108, 117–129, 130, 131, 132, 133, 134, 138, 139, 144, 150, 151, 152, 154, 158, 160, 162
  Verbal illumination, 108, 118–119, 121, 128
  Rhythmical illumination, 57n, 108, 118–122, 128
Imagination, 2, 12, 28, 29, 155, 170, 170n
"Imminence", 112n, 127n
"Implexe, l'", 54–55, 87
"Improvisation de degré supérieur", 111–116, 140n, 146, 155, 163
Incubation, 116, 128
"Indivisibles", 42, 47, 48
Inspiration, (definition), 5–9

'Total inspiration', 6, 11, 12, 18, 32, 34, 77, 104, 116, 167
'Intermittent inspiration', 7, 8, 9, 18, 20, 68, 69–71, 77, 102, 115, 126, 167; see "poetic state"
'Intuitive inspiration', 7, 8, 9, 18, 20, 77, 102, 108, 116, 126, 129, 151, 154, 160, 167; see illumination
'Exalted inspiration', 8, 9, 18, 20, 77, 112, 114, 115, 131, 146, 162, 167; see "improvisation de degré supérieur"
'Attributed inspiration', 8, 18, 89–94, 167
'Personal inspiration', 9, 18, 20, 138, 164–177
Intellect, 4, 14, 17, 25, 26, 29, 30, 38, 39, 41, 43, 44, 51, 58, 59, 60, 61, 65, 75, 77–89, 104–106, 125, 128, 164, 165, 169, 170, 176n
"Intimation", 96, 96n, 117, 127–129, 132–136, 138–140, 140n, 141–142, 144, 149–151, 153
Introduction à la méthode de Léonard de Vinci, 14–18, 19–20.

Jeune Parque, La, 27, 31, 66n, 68, 79, 85, 97, 116, 116n, 156, 159, 159n, 160, 161, 164, 167
Jones, P. M., vii
Jones, R. S., 21

Lafont, A., 174n
Lamartine, 4
Language, 60, 67, 84–86, 91–92, 107
Latour, J. de, 35
Le Breton, G., 37n
Leduc, Madame, vii
Leonardo da Vinci, 15, 17, 18, 22, 23, 24, 25, 45, 53, 54n, 109
Lewis, C. Day, 19
Louÿs, P., 16n, 42n, 109, 145n, 160

MacNeice, L., 19
Mallarmé, 5, 12, 20, 22, 24, 26, 74, 74*n*, 75, 76, 87*n*, 112, 152, 166, 173
Mathematics, 15, 22, 23*n*, 169
Maxwell, Clerk, 23, 23*n*
Mechanistic viewpoint, 18, 42
Mécs, L., 115
"Mental sets", 52–54, 106
Mental association, 2, 170
Metaphors, 82, 147–148
Modern Language Review, 21*n*
"Moi complet, le", 82, 87, 126, 147, 148
"Moi instantané, le" ("moi de l'instant", "moi fonctionnel"), 47–48, 50, 52, 54, 82, 87, 107, 126, 131, 147, 148
"Moi pur, le," 26*n*, 30, 107; *see* 'awareness'
"Monde de l'attention, le", *see* "la phase"
Mondor, H., 11*n*, 16*n*, 152, 173*n*
Monod, J., 23*n*
Morality, 60, 169
Moral values of poetic composition, 66–67
Moreau, P., vii
Morris, W., 9
Mysticism, 22
Mystique, 12–14, 17, 25–26, 45, 59, 64–65, 96, 112, 125
Myths, 59–61, 66, 82, 90, 94, 106

Nadal, O., vii, 13, 14, 15, 24*n*, 29, 94*n*, 154*n*, 173*n*
Napoleon, 22
Narcisse, 26
Nervous energy, 56–57, 60, 61, 88
Nervous system, 35–63, 77–89
Newton, 2, 52
Noulet, E., 24*n*, 146

"Objective correlatives", 137

"Obstacles" during composition, 151–154
Organic process of creation, 2, 3, 170

Palme, 116
Pascal, 104
Pattern given by illumination, 134, 138
Period of silence, Valéry's, 25, 64, 96, 173
"Phase, la," 56, 78, 86
Physical sciences, 2
Physics, 28–29, 45, 115*n*
Physiology, 35, 40–43, 43*n*, 44–62, 71, 80, 93, 170
Planck, Max, 28
Plato, 1, 3, 4
Plotinus, 4
Poe, E. A., 11, 12, 14, 16, 20, 24, 33, 66*n*, 69, 74, 76, 97, 157, 173
"Poetic state", 6–7, 8, 69–72, 100, 101, 104, 108, 117–129, 130, 131, 167
Poetry, (nature, functions and personal ideal), 69–76
Poincaré, H., 21–23, 23*n*, 24, 139, 139*n*
Pope, 2
Preparation of poet, 51, 96–117, 127, 129
Proliferation, 121, 127–128, 149, 156
Prose, (nature and functions), 72, 73
Psychiatry, 45, 169
Psychology, 12, 14, 16, 17, 35, 36, 40, 43*n*, 45, 62, 64, 71, 81*n*, 93, 158, 169, 170
"Pure poetry", 73–76, 94*n*, 95, 152, 153, 163
Pythie, La, 68
Raine, K., 134*n*
Raymond, M., 125, 174*n*, 176*n*
Read, H., 9
Reality, conception of, 46–47, 52–53

"Refusals", 139, 163
Relationships, 17, 21–23, 28, 97
Relativity, 28, 29
Relaxed consciousness, 125, 141–142
Resonance, 70, 77, 81, 83, 85, 87, 100, 109, 123
Rhythms, 7, 50, 71, 79, 83, 86, 92
Ribot, Th., 125
Richards, I. A., 48, 50, 66
Rimbaud, 26, 173, 173n
Robinson, J., 21n
Romantic poets, 3–5, 11, 32, 95, 101–102, 105

Saint-Exupéry, 175
Scarfe, F., 123n
Schiller, 134n
Schrödinger, 28
Science, scientific thought, 15, 21–25, 27–31, 38, 46, 65–66, 97, 98, 169
Self, the, 36, 176
  Gulf between self and reality, 26–27, 174, 175–177
  Multiplicity of self, selves, 52, 86, 101, 107, 109, 109n
  Two selves of Valéry, 68, 175
  See "moi complet", "moi in-stantané", "moi pur"
Self-knowledge, 15, 17, 19, 20, 24, 26, 66–67, 96, 99, 117
Sensations, 37, 43, 45, 48, 48n, 49, 49n, 50, 50n, 51, 54, 56, 82, 87, 106, 107, 147, 148
  Motor sensations, 50, 51, 55, 83
Sense impressions, 2, 170
Sensibility, 30, (definition) 37, 37n, 38–39, 41, 43, 43n, 44, 47, 48, 49, 50, 51, 52, 61, 61n, 62, 65, 70, 71, 75, 78, 79, 86, 88, 101, 101n, 103–106, 106n, 107, 108, 109, 114, 125, 126, 128, 131, 137, 144, 146, 152, 155, 165, 169, 170, 170n
Servien, P., 104, 114
Shelley, 3, 4, 32

Skelton, R., 134n, 138
Soirée avec Monsieur Teste, La, 14–15, 17, 19, 24, 44
Solipsism, 15, 16n, 47
Spire, A., 142
Subconscious, the, 6, 143, 170n, 174n
Suckling, N., 171
Supernatural, 6, 32, 89
Sur la technique littéraire, 11–14, 18–19
Surrealism, 171
Sutcliffe, F. E., 21n, 22n, 23n, 29n
Swedenborg, 52, 57, 85
Sykes, L. C., vii

Technique, 4, (definition) 5–6, 9–20, 24, 26, 31, 33, 34, 35, 38, 47, 62, 63, 64, 89, 91–94, 95, 104, 110, 166–168, 169, 174
"Tempérament poétique essentiel, le", 100–101
Tendencies in previous poets carried further by Valéry, 68, 76, 79, 103, 117, 131, 167, 171
Teste, Monsieur, 17, 18, 22, 23, 25, 26, 93, 146
Thomson, J. J., 28
"Thresholds, mental", 59–61, 79, 81, 82, 83, 169
Time factor in nervous system, 48, 52, 81, 83, 111
Trahard, P., 157
Transcendence, 3, 4, 8, 13, 14, 15, 24, 71, 90, 175, 177
Transitions in poetry, 161

Unconscious, the, 3, 4, 6, 108n, 141, 141n
Unconscious (-ly), 4, 5, 6, 58, 68, 124, 125, 133, 150, 170, 171
Universal knowledge, 24–26, 33, 40, 64, 112
Universal mind, 13, 15, 18, 22–23, 30, 46, 109

"Vague, le", 22, 59, 61n, 62, 170
Valéry, Claude,   23n
Valéry, Jules,   43
Valéry, Madame,   vii, 62n
Verification,   139
Verlaine,   11
"Vers donnés, trouvés", 150, 150n,
    153, 154, 158
"Vers faits, calculés", 150, 150n, 151

Viennese Circle,   60n
Wahl, J.,   176n
Wallas, G., 96, 96n, 116, 139, 139n,
    140
Wittgenstein,   60n
"Worlds" of sensibility,   49, 88
"Worlds" of poetry,   70, 107
Yggdrasill,   37n